Ideas of Order

Also by David Lindley

POETRY
Poems
The Night Outside
Five, Seven, Five
Something & Nothing: Selected Poems

PROSE
The Freedom to Be Tragic

IDEAS OF ORDER

David Lindley

We are the bees of the invisible.
Rainer Maria Rilke

Verborum Editions

First published 2009 by Verborum Editions
Reset and reprinted 2013

Verborum Editions
5 Lauds Road
Crick
Northamptonshire
England
NN6 7TJ

www.verborumeditions.com

Set in Janson

Book designed by Sarah Rock

978-1-907100-00-0

PROLOGUE

*Perhaps as an adjunct to his person, perhaps
to compensate for his dullness, the bowerbird
of New Guinea collects colourful objects and
makes pleasing arrangements of them at the
threshold of his bower. Among the objects of
his attention are stones, fruits, shells, bones,
mushrooms, beetle skeletons, fresh flowers
and, from time to time, shotgun cartridges
discarded by that other and more mindful
collector, man.*

*There is in this habit, one supposes, some
deep and unavoidable imperative that has
the appearance of order and purpose. On
the other hand, none of it makes sense. This
miscellaneous lapidary collection of discoveries
has no meaning, or at least no meaning
beyond what he finds significant that he is
pleased to occupy himself with.*

1

*Philosophical syntheses and ethical
systems are only possible in arm-chair
moments. They are seen to be meaningless
as soon as we get into a bus with a
dirty baby and a crowd.*

T E Hulme

Begin with experience.

One must begin, here, with consciousness, without proposing a first cause or principle, without asking for anything.

You can't work back from the given to the giver.

To be and to cease to be must be enough.

You cannot get out of experience something beyond experience.

Nothing can be understood outside the present moment. Therefore the profoundest truths can be mentioned only in passing.

Experience does not extend beyond sensibility, ideas do not range beyond intelligibility.

To conceive of the world in my absence it is necessary for me to be present.

I try to hold in my mind the whole nexus of history, past and to come, and to do it justice, as though the whole of eternity had eyes and was watching. But only I am watching. My life is precisely this contingency, this accident of being. I sit before an open window. Once it is closed, I have no part in anything.

A life is a point of view.

The search for a supreme idea in which all our anxieties will come to rest is a hopeless quest to find a mythical creature invented by anxiety itself.

All our questions about the nature of the world are really questions about the nature of our own discomfort.

Where, I ask with the Pythagoreans and with Kant, are the triangles of experience?

Nowhere in the world is a single idea to be found.

Life is in the detail, the concrete, the particular.

Nothing is dependent on its explanation.

We possess this life that is utterly unique, yet we despair in the search for universal principles.

Why should the world be *subject* to the intellect?

My conscious life is my only life, my consciousness of the world is the only knowledge of the world I can have. If there were another and a better world beyond my experience, it could not matter to me, and if I were to form an idea of it, then the form of the idea would immediately become the form of that world, subsumed once more into my consciousness.

What, then, is my unconscious life? Something my conscious life knows about. How else could I have written this down?

What is the unknown? Something I know.

The mind, *and nothing else*, illumines the world.

Thought is a tool for action. It's the axe that breaks the ice so we can let down a line for the fish we know are under there.

Thought models experience. It is able to do this *in the absence of direct experience*. Our thoughts are models of our understanding and not models of the world.

The shapes of our thoughts are the shapes of our potential actions and the shapes of things themselves are the shapes of our potential actions upon them.

Creatures who are simply aware of the flow of sensations live entirely in the present. Their actions are *integral* actions *in* not *upon* experience.

Animals do not know themselves, therefore they cannot choose to be less than perfect. But we, as soon as we recognise ourselves, falter.

Integral actions are unknown actions, unknown to the one that acts.

What is not known is unknowable.

What is the form of the external world? Not the form constructed by our thinking, but its unknowable form.

Nature is nature, it knows nothing.

The real world, in fact, is lost to its description.

All other creatures have a wisdom for the present moment only. But we remember, so the moment does not pass away but is woven into a narrative of past and future. So, for example, the transformation of the seasons from spring to summer is a hidden phenomenon revealed solely through the act of remembering. Our thoughts are the secrets of nature.

The inner landscape is the one we are born to, into which we are entirely absorbed. The outer, the other landscape, is the emptiness, the absence of ourselves into which we vanish.

If the impulse of my will can move my arm so effortlessly, can shift my gaze so easily, how much more easily might I not will the world into being, which is a matter of mere perception, and so perfectly that I am unaware that I do it?

It is impossible for us to separate the world from our consciousness of it.

To feel that one's life is somehow *meant* is the first and least susceptible to doubt of all our illusions.

If you insist there is nothing to be revealed, only illusions to be got rid of, no one will believe you. Everyone will prefer to believe there is something behind your back. Confronted by this sort of obtuseness it becomes more and more difficult not to be misrepresented. Language is driven to become cryptic. In the end one has to be content with silence to avoid making an enigma out of nothing.

A coherent discourse requires a rational argument. If the natural order of things is incoherent, what can we say about it?

Silence, unfortunately, serves both ignorance and understanding.

Silence can't exist without a word for silence.

We can't say for certain that order is present in nature, because we can find order only in the act of observing order, and what we observe is the mind's idea of order. Order is really *ordering*, what the mind imposes on emptiness, silence, incoherence.

Order is for expediency of action. It's the rough sorting of phenomena so that experience is never just one thing after another. If you take away mental categories, experience really is just one damned thing after another.

To define is to break apart. What cannot be broken apart remains undefined.

Some of our first thoughts were stones.

Pain and consciousness share a history. We suffer in order to be. We cannot have knowledge without the anxiety of what we know.

We know in order to escape the bondage of paradise, that garden of unknowing. But knowledge is guilt. We are uncertain of who it is we have betrayed.

Except for suffering we could know nothing.

Without the excitation of the nervous system the brain could not have evolved. Without pain we could not have arrived at consciousness. We inherit suffering when we inherit freedom.

So what do you want to be – unchanging matter, a stick, a stone?

There is no reality without mind.

The reintegration of experience and intuition requires a suspension of abstraction, analysis, reduction, the habit of breaking down experience into sequential, causative, component parts; the suspension of insecurity and our fear of falling; and of that most essential, fond, useful concept of the self as initiator, observer, controller, who must be subsumed into the act itself.

We think we are the subject, but are we? Are we not simply the *object* of a multitude of particles following their own course, like light through a prism?

Subject and object, seer and seen, they are the same continuous flux of matter floating through space, like shattered fragments of a mirror.

Reality is an accidental by-product of the evolution of consciousness.

Reality, that immovable presence, is the affliction of consciousness.

We are shut out from unthinking life. We are men, not dogs.

In order to make sense of things our mind perpetually closes down on every experience in judgment. Everything that is, *is* by virtue of being judged to be.

As soon as we differentiate we judge.

Reality *is* thinking.

The natural order of the world is its unknowable order. Its knowable order is its useful order.

Understanding is preparation for action.

There are many contingent necessities for understanding, but there is no *absolute* necessity either for understanding or for explanation.

Understanding is essentially a mechanism for survival for creatures burdened with consciousness.

Order is the first requirement of understanding.

The act of ordering requires a capacity for ordering. The existence of a capacity for ordering implies the existence of *pre-ordinate generalities* into which particulars will fit.

There is nothing intrinsic in particulars characteristic of a general category unless we can first conceive of a general category out of which we can distribute intrinsic characteristics.

Order has its origins in the incipient logical forms of behavioural responses.

The act of perception itself is the cause of the order we perceive.

Natural order is its unperceived order.

Meaning is the recognition of order.

Science can only reveal those things that we have already imagined.

Science *began* as poetry. It fails to sustain us now only because it insists on reducing the adventures of human imagination to mere facts in the external world, *aliena*, as Traherne says, not of ourselves. But it is of ourselves.

Science has a limited number of tasks to perform. It acts in the light of the possible; it does not reconcile us to the impossible.

The mind will have to think its way back into its evolutionary origins if it wishes to understand itself.

The self is the satellite of the other, whirled in its orbit.

When finally mind is reduced to not-mind, with what shall we think about it?

When the evolutionary role of mind is finally understood science will restore our capacity to see God, for it will restore the legitimacy of the imagination.

And what is God but the other clothed in the mystery and splendour of the self?

And God said, Because I can do everything, I must do nothing.

Nouns appear to be simple things, but they are full of our intentions, interests and suspicions.

Language itself, in the simplest conceptual forms of subject, verb, object, holds the key to the operation of consciousness upon the integrity of experience.

Experience and language are inextricable.

Language makes absolute the merely convenient.

Reason should be seen as part of our *physiological* nature.

Reason is an offensive weapon, sharper and much bloodier than tooth and claw.

Reasoning is only one activity of the mind, but the one that has proved to be the most practically useful. For all its apparent abstraction reason is firmly rooted in biological necessity.

When our heart fails us we lose our animal nature, when our reason fails us we lose our human nature.

The mind is an extension of interestedness that is inherent in every organism. It sees what it is interested in seeing. The mind functions within the limits of self-interest.

The sea anemone knows nothing of the moon, yet the tides sustain it. What is it that *we* don't know?

What is understood is dependent on what is not understood.

We can find reasons for everything, but nothing is *founded* on reason.

When we get below the surface, to the root of it all, there is enlightenment, but no light. Light is all above, darkness below. Our roots are in the deepest dark.

Instinct and reason are matters of degree not kind. Reason has grown in us like the exaggerated antennae of some blind insect. We cannot escape from reason, for reason is in the nature of the beast.

A reason for being that is outside being could only be arrived at from the point of view of non-being, which is impossible. The reason for being can only be found in (a) reason, (b) being.

We look for reasons *because* we have the power of reasoning.

The mechanism of evolution by which we have arrived at being, and the mechanism of consciousness through which the world has translated itself into reality, are only mechanisms. Understanding what those mechanisms are does not lessen the reality of the real or detract from the experience of being. It changes nothing.

The world lends me my mind, my mind lends it meaning.

There is meaning in the world, but it does not touch it.

The absolute is a word among words.

Reality is ours and, it must be understood, *only* ours.

My sense of reality *is* reality. Reality is entirely inner, realisation entirely inward.

To answer the question, What is reality? you have to answer the question, What is realisation? – this apparent simultaneity of the world and its representation.

There is no reality beyond realisation. What is beyond realisation is empty, nameless, void, unknowable.

Our sense of reality is our sense of being.

Being is knowing.

Only the unknowing are perfect in their own natures. Nothing in the natural world can ever be anything less than itself.

'Reality' isn't 'hard'. That sort of 'objective' reality is really the absence of reality, the blind banging of an armoured woodlouse against the tiles, wandering in and out of darkness on the bathroom floor.

If we were perfect we would have no desires. And what do we desire most but something lost, a lost contentment, the recovery of which alone will put an end to our desires?

We have no *natural* place in the world. We arrive here as the fox does and the squirrel, but as aliens. They have their fox natures and squirrel natures in which they dwell unquestioningly. But we become ourselves only by an act of imagination. For us, human nature is not an answer but an unanswerable question.

Although we have lost our first innocence, that knowledge that is no knowledge, the knowledge of how to act without acting, to do without doing, that state of perfection without doubt of every adapted creature not stricken with consciousness, we would never surrender our consciousness. We are fatally committed to our illusions. Perfection and the absence of doubt belong to the abyss, to unconscious nature. It is our nature to derive from experience our sustaining illusions and, in the final analysis, to find ourselves worthy of them.

For us, knowledge is destiny.

The mystery that can never be revealed to us is the possibility of being without knowledge of being.

The very concept of reality is a statement about consciousness.

It is in the activity of the mind, in the realm of thought, that we really have our being.

Questions of reality have nothing whatever to do with questions of whether the world really exists.

If God is the answer, he is also the question.

We ask why in the name of God, but answer in the name of man, who has a few tricks up his sleeve.

The one who has the answer to this knot of complexities is the one who made it.

If we admit that questions can be framed only in the mind, why then do we make the mistake of believing that legitimate answers can lie outside it, as though answers stood independent and alone, absolute, objective, external, and were not themselves the self-absorbed reflections of the questioning mind?

Questions posed by the intellect are answered by a reformulation of the conceptual language of the intellect, much as propositions in mathematics are resolved in mathematical language. Answers to questions posed in one language and responded to in another will always appear irrational since, by definition, intellectual language is rational language. Intuitive language and experiential language offer alternative responses whose essential characteristic is surprise. An indecent proposal receives a slap in the face, the sound of one hand clapping is heard in the sudden crowing of a cockerel in a distant farmyard.

The question is the question, the problem is the problem. The question is resolved by the answer, the problem by the solution. But what remains to be answered is why the question arose and how the problem came to be. By formulating *that* question and the answer that will resolve it, I yet manage to leave the question open, for the question of the question remains. The child's question, 'Why?' to every answer illustrates the interrogative condition of the species, a condition not mended by any conceivable answer to any conceivable question. None of the questions in the childish chain of endless regression addresses the interrogative condition itself, and when it is formulated – 'Why am I asking this question?' – it remains a symptom of the condition. It follows that the question of the question and the problem of the problem cannot be resolved by answers formulated in the same condition as the question. The answers must be sought outside the locked room of our malady, written in another hand. It is as though we were to ask a question in English and one day find by way of an answer a letter delivered containing a poem in Chinese, or we posed a mathematical problem and the answer arrived on our doorstep in an empty box wrapped in brown paper.

The great unanswered 'why' question is the why 'why' question.

There is only one unanswerable riddle in the universe – why being and not nothingness is its ruling principle.

Meaning only matters *because* meaning matters. Its origin should be sought among the sources of other irritations.

Looking backward, our lives will always seem to have been meant. But if we try to imagine ourselves looking forward with the blind eye of the hydrogen atom, we fail. Nothing was meant, nothing was inevitable.

Human sentience and consciousness are a fact. There is nothing to be added to it by recasting that fact as *nothing but* another fact.

Books, Rilke remarks, break off pieces of the world, until it is all in fragments. The world is whole only in the absence of our knowledge of it.

To arrive at understanding one first breaks up what has been given as a whole. The secret of the universe, we imagine, is in there somewhere. To accept it as a gift is not enough. We tip out the world like the contents of a birthday watch on a sheet of newspaper on the kitchen table. From the complexity of parts we construct a theory of the whole. If the theory is valid it will tick to our satisfaction, and what we shall have in the end is what we had in the beginning but could not accept unconditionally. The world is the world, and a theory of the world is a theory of the world, an arabesque.

All conclusions are stepping stones to the great conclusion that lies across the abyss.

When I say 'I understand' I imply that I have just solved a puzzle. But since there never was a puzzle, what is it that I have understood? What understanding understands is understanding itself: not what something is, but what someone is saying about something, what I myself am saying about something; not in the language of being, but in a language 'about' being.

Reason pushed to its limits will always give way to the irrational.

Why would we wish to be remembered merely for our usefulness?

After all, the only possible conclusion is the one that leaves open all possible conclusions.

Philosophical truth is a habit of reflection taken to an obsessive extreme of inclusiveness.

Unity is unity of thought. Philosophy is really a passion for tidiness, an anxiety about order.

There is no philosophy apart from the philosopher.

The philosopher, in the quiet of his study, cannot encompass in his thought the cry of a child in the night in another part of the city, nor the thoughts of the mother awakened by the crying child, neither the immediacy of experience nor the reality that for her is the most immediate and real of experiences. Philosophy embraces nothing wider than the immediate experience of thinking. That a thought may hold the world together in some sort of sublime thematic unity is a proposition thwarted by the cry of a child, an illusion contradicted by the impossibility that there ever could be, within an all inclusive philosophy, inclusiveness of experience.

No philosopher *reluctantly* accepts his own theory. His theory is complete when he is satisfied with it.

Philosophy is to be stepped over.

Ideas were first a hunter's dream. Now they are set loose and stalk the world.

Once we have seized hold of the idea of perfection the world must look out, for in the idea of perfection lies the idea of the world's imperfection, the fault in creation, the crack in the teacup.

We intellectualise a world that has no thought content in it whatsoever.

We are beguiled by our own abilities to reason.

Ideas hunt their origins.

All forms of tyranny are firstly tyrannies of the mind.

Abstract man is the darling of the state. He is the man of philosophers, moralists, reformers, unifiers and revolutionaries. He is the ideal man, the imagined, the dreamed, the unreal. He is the unrealised and unrealisable. But it is precisely for the sake of the unrealised man, the man of the future, that the man of flesh and bone, the man of here and now, is sacrificed.

The individual is the last barrier against evil.

Act against evil, do nothing for good.

The worst imaginable horror is finding yourself an alien in the ideology and theology of complete strangers, like the American Indians who were taken to be the lost tribe of Israel and punished for past sins of which they were unaware.

Ethical values are rooted in aesthetic values.

There is no value in human consciousness without the admission of common humanity.

We derive our ethical responsibilities out of the exercise of our aesthetic responsibilities, and we derive our aesthetic responsibilities from the absolute value of consciousness.

The best idea is to have no ideas.

A theory that survives doubt will not survive certainty.

Making up our minds is the most foolish thing we ever do.

Experience is heretic.

The question, Does the bird know it is singing? can just as easily be reformulated as, Does the singing know it's a bird?

Grand designs are built on *principles*. It is only at the smallest everyday level that we are in touch with *experience*.

Nothing is so small it can't contain the whole universe.

The function of society is to provide the individual with the means by which he may escape from it.

There is a progress of knowledge but not a progress of experience.

The individual carries the burden of consciousness for the sake of the whole world.

It is not enough for the world simply to be: it must be narrated. The myths of creation are no mere pre-scientific explanations of a world deemed simply to be. They are the assertion of our responsibility for the act of creation, of the primacy of myth itself, of consciousness above chaos, of narrative above incoherence.

As a matter of fact, the process of maturation serves only self-renewal. The significance of life lies always in its beginnings not in its maturity, in the pupal stage of expectation, in metamorphosis.

Anyway, our lives began as someone else's fictions...

The individual is a paradox of self and other. The process of individuation requires of the self the absorption within it of all other selves, of all past lives, all of mortality, all suffering. In fact it requires total self-identification with the human condition. The self that rises above all other selves, that grasps the illusion of power, does so only by putting off all sense of the common condition. In the act of seeking power, true selfhood is abandoned. In attempting to substantiate itself by seeking power over others, the self *becomes* the other, the alien, the outcast, the inhuman.

Poetry is the only true exercise of power.

Poetry is a stronger illusion than power, because power has no source in experience. The desire for power grows out of the poverty of the self.

There is no last word. Objectivity has the authority of reason, but reason holds its authority only in the absence of a greater power.

Reason, too, must be judged.

Reality is individual conscious experience.

How carefully one watches determines what happens in the world. Only our simple acts of affirmation make existence possible.

Mind and creative mind are not distinct.

We see what we imagine we see. It is our fate to be tellers of tales.

To be requires no justification.

Consciousness is our reason for being.

Our reason for being does not presuppose intentionality.

Our reason for being is not the world's reason for our being.

Only our reason requires reasons.

Realisation of the real is responsibility for the real. I do not mean this simply as an obligation, but as a matter of fact.

Being is the realisation of being; the realisation of being gives us power over the real; when we have power over the real we acquire responsibility for the real.

Reflection is an act of passion not an act of reason.

The truth is not obscure, just surprising.

It is the ordinary, common, everyday world that is utterly incomprehensible.

For the most part we inhabit our conscious world in much the same way as a fish swims in the sea, at one with its medium. Only occasionally do we suddenly recognise the extraordinariness of our situation, much as a fish, as it hits the deck, might in its last gasp of unaccustomed air recognise the wordless incomprehensibility of the ordinary.

To be certain, to believe a singularity, to be without perplexity, is to be imprisoned in a tower without a door, with only a narrow window to look out of upon a kingdom that once was ours.

Wisdom is poor recompense for not having lived.

The innocent dwell in infinity, the wise are walled in stone.

Other people's truths are dreary things.

My fictions are my realities.

The more elegant an idea, the more likely we are to be convinced by it. Truth is an aspect of aesthetics.

We are magicians. We conjure with the real – *pragmatisti magica*, as Papini says.

Illusion is the language of being.

The difference between reality and imagination is just a matter of its urgency.

The real is the imagined gnawed by anxiety.

The objective, too, can only be imagined.

What is the self but theatre?

To celebrate the world is to celebrate myself.

Don't tell me my idea of reality is an illusion. I know it. I revel in it.

We find our consolation in the lives we have already lived.

We read in the hope of stumbling upon some fellow we recognise.

What we look for in our heroes is the triumph of the imagination.

Ah, if only life *were* all explanation.

A life is to be expended, not preserved.

When all has been said, what shall we say? When all has been done, what shall we do? Live, for example?

Survival is nothing, it is merely evasion. Realisation is everything.

We strive to preserve something that will signify our lives, yet even in its sublimity that significance can only ever be a shadow of the fullness of a life, an actual life, a life ultimately disregarded, sacrificed and subordinated to the imagined tyrant who demands a reason for our being, when in fact what our fate requires of us is a life lived.

The lived life has no summing up

One would suppose that the measure of truth would be its self-sufficiency. Why, then, must it be *told?* Perhaps we are less interested in the truth than in distinguishing ourselves.

No story ends better than it begins. No reward of heaven will ever compensate us for loss of earth.

Satisfaction doesn't satisfy.

Our lives are an infinite series of beginnings that no imagined ending can ever satisfy.

Heaven is nothing to us, less than nothing, worse than death. Only the struggle towards heaven matters to us, only the fight against death.

Solutions mark the limits of our imagination.

We must look for solutions in terms of satisfactions, in terms of their consolation, and not in terms of truth.

What we should work towards is imaginative fulfilment, not ultimate solutions. We have heard enough already of final solutions.

The truths we are happiest with are not those we discover but those we remember.

Make no mistake – meaning is entirely to be discovered in our own lived lives and not in any larger universal principle.

One of the great fundamental errors of our thinking lies in the separation of substance and attribute. This arbitrary division is reinforced by language, and has become the rule of law. To break this law is the first act of freedom.

No one thing corresponds with any other. An observation is one thing – it does not correspond with the thing observed.

That truth is what appears to be true most of the time to most of the people who are most reasonable falls short of most people's idea of truth.

The truth of science is the common ground of methodology. The truth of poetry is realisation.

The imagination is limited only by its vocabulary.

We cannot return to wholeness through reason, since it was reason alone that determined our separateness.

There is no 'whole', no 'one' to which we can return. We are exiles. All our knowledge of life is on this side of the divide.

In no creation myth do we find that first their was reason and *then* God.

Unlike poetry and religion, music has to be excused its irrationality by the defenders of reason. Its mystery is credited with more sublimity than the idea of God. As though Bach should have written a mass for the dinosaurs.

The natural state of an idea is one of suspended anxiety, resolved only by the satisfaction of experience.

The more we feel we are alien in the world the clearer does it become that our anxiety is resolved only by an act of *recognition*. Solutions may appear to be worked out by reason, but the measure of any solution is its satisfaction. The fact that reasoned solutions are *satisfying* gives reason the power it has over our minds. Satisfaction, not reason, provides us with answers. The solution to every problem is a kind of homecoming. The more alien we feel, the more anxious we are to find what we believe we have lost, a familiar door left open for us. Behind that door, in the perspective of biology, is my mother; in the light of evolution, my original nature; to my imagination, God; in reality, myself.

Purpose, in the end, will never prove to be more than the aesthetically pleasing, meaning, more than that which satisfies.

Order satisfies.

Our thoughts have no more profundity than our sexual desires. Our sexual satisfactions are sufficient to themselves. Our certainties, too, are, as it were, small orgasmic satisfactions of the mind.

We arrive inevitably at the point where love is the only certainty.

Being is in perception and realisation, in inexplicable aesthetic satisfactions. It irritates that they remain unexplained to the divided self that will be content only with reasons.

Aesthetic judgments are absolute judgments: 'and God saw that it was good.'

Even when we turn our minds to God we can think of nothing higher than being and the realisation of being.

Philosophy pursues last things but poetry is content with first things.

Reasoning will take you back to the foundation of reason, but no amount of reasoning will take you *beyond* the foundation of reason. There are *ultimate facts* that lie outside the order of reason.

If reason isn't the answer, reasoning that it isn't, isn't. We must do something else.

The limits of language mark the boundaries of coherence.

Without language we would possess only an astonished silence.

Reason presents us with an infinite number of ways of losing ourselves. We must endeavour to find our way back through the dark wood of abstraction.

The world is intelligible to the intelligence. It has no intelligibility *beyond* the intelligence.

Intellectualism is a fabrication, a sham.

What ultimately we are satisfied with are nothing less than those former things of wordless and thought-free contentment displaced by the necessity of thinking.

Thought will always shape itself to our heart's affections.

Meaning lies in the self-sufficiency of the mind's idea of order.

Solutions are always aesthetic solutions.

If God is my heart's desire, why should I surrender my heart's desire to mere reason?

Our belief in immortality, in personal survival, is the assertion of a value against which we measure all our values.

What is it that we have lost at the centre of our being, in this the most tragic of centuries, or, rather, what is it we have accepted as our true natures, if, confronted with ultimate horror, we turn away from ultimate seriousness content with two or three conventional phrases, the idea of personal happiness, and the sufficiency of tambourines as the summation of belief?

Whether by accident, as we now surmise, or by design, as we once believed, we have risen from zygotic blindness to question the profound mystery of our being, and we have no alternative but to answer with our own voice.

Living is an act of faith. Reasons always run out.

Love is the worst of words. When someone uses it you can't imagine what they might have meant by it.

A poem is a way of proceeding.

A prayer, a song, a chant, the poem itself – aren't these the necessary obligations to the world of living and being to which we are devoted?

When we understand, we will understand that we are all artists. What sort of artist is a matter of temperament. We may listen to this rhapsody, 'the rhapsody of things as they are,' or, like the dreaming Chinese poet, take to horse, to action and to battle, for this is also the human sphere, all of it, all of it.

If art baffles, then it baffles only that habit of mind that values analysis above creation. The danger of too much explanation is in seeing more in the unravelling than in the making.

Art, to be art, must contain some element of the impossible.

Revelation in art is always imminent.

Art is realisation through equivalence.

The perfect poem holds fast to its origins in sensibility. It must exhibit the roots of its perceptual beginnings and the form of its unattainable ends.

A poem is a strange new form of order.

In the practical sphere there are no mysteries, only in the analytical sphere. No amount of analysis will get to the heart of why language works in a poem. The structures, tones, cadences, resonances only describe what is happening. How satisfaction inheres in a line of a poem is of the same order of mysteriousness as how beauty comes to be inherent in truth. The question will always take us straight back to the aesthetics of order, which seems to be an absolute beyond which there is only that sort of futile speculation we indulge in about the outer limits of eternity.

Things take the forms of our potential actions upon them. But the forms of things are also the forms of our celebration of them. We not only know them in an intuitive way and in a rational way (their functional forms) but also in an entirely *irrelevant* way (their aesthetic forms.) Aesthetic forms are the forms of our affections. Art is a refusal to surrender the forms of our affections to the functional forms of necessity.

What are the forms of art? The forms of celebration. What are the forms of celebration? The forms of our affections. What are the forms of our affections? The 'brick walls, blank windows, old clothes' that Turner saw from his window.

Art is not a point of view, it is not opinion.

The modes of thought are just as much a matter of character and inclination and first affections as the modes of art.

Even Christ had only one idea.

Time? We inhabit levels of the soul, we enter certain realms. The soul has many layers, we ascend and descend on ladders, like angels.

Time running out creates the greatest of our anxieties. But time does not run out.

It is life, not death, that always takes us by surprise.

We fear death itself less than we fear the failure of ambition and hope.

If we strive all our lives to be remembered, what is the point of that? It means some other life must be spent in striving to remember us. What, then, becomes the point of that life? No. Each life is a window opened, then closed. It is of this moment, it has no cumulative significance. Maybe we feel entrusted with something, something entrusted, perhaps, as Rilke thought, not to the most suitable person. But there is no one acting on our behalf. This all happens just once, contingently. We find comfort in remembering those who were here before us. That we acknowledge the concreteness of their former presence is of no comfort to *them*.

The praise of one's contemporaries seems like a foretaste of immortality. But it is only a widening of one's own emptiness: 'Young man anywhere, in whom something is welling up that makes you shiver, be grateful that no one knows you.'

All acts of creation arise out of self-doubt.

We can do nothing nobler with our lives than serve our noblest fictions.

One must strive to say as little as possible.

To write like this is to compact all thought into sweet or bitter pills, like those 'paper pills' of Doctor Reefy in Sherwood Anderson's Winesburg Ohio, screwed up paper pellets of thinking, the taste of existence from instant to instant.

Philosophising is economy of effort. Most of what we think, know or believe can be summed up as: the virtue of being human is the ability to wonder that the world is as it is and not otherwise. The poet's task is similarly economical, but, none the less, he has to hunt down additional words and fix the wonder in a particular experience and make it general. The writer's task, otherwise, is prolix. For that sort of writer, it is not enough that the street outside is as it is – all of it, and all possibilities of it, have to be described, so that we wonder at it. It's all a matter of temperament, a preference for shortcuts or thoroughness.

Always the most important things are those that are unsaid.

We can succeed in one thing only by failing at something else.

All successes are successes within limits.

I write for myself, for the self that lives through ages, to sustain unbroken the line that connects my past to my future, from age to age, in order not to fail myself. It is more important to do this than to be admired.

We seek praise and admiration out of fear, fear of the solitude and silence of the self.

The self has no companions.

The real has its ciphers for this and that, and this and that are what we follow, what we desire and what we seize upon (the sky, for convenience, is always blue.) But the real is the realised, the realised the real, and so inevitably we drift apart, you to your blue heaven and I to mine.

More and more I am convinced we strive simply to go home. What we desire most is less some never to be achieved fulfilment than the recovery of lost contentment. We look for the key to a locked door, we search for a room in a house we know, a forgotten street in a familiar town, 'the lost lane-end into Heaven.'

Absolute truth is absolute consolation.

2

The idiom of order is celebration.

W S Merwin

Our only measure of truth is the extent to which what we have put in order satisfies our sense of what order itself is.

There is nothing intrinsically desirable in any object. Nor, by the same token, is order exemplified in any object of our attention. Just as desire itself makes things desirable, so our attention lends order. We think we see order, as we think we see colour, in the object of our attention, where in fact it is we ourselves, the 'bees of the invisible,' who make order visible.

To write is to create order. To write more is to impose more order, to work towards some sort of finality or completeness, the ordering of my thoughts to an ideal of inclusiveness. To write less, to write the least and, if one could forego the vanity of ambition, to write not at all, would give one an even chance of evading the definitive and the conclusive.

We are dependent on those who have preceded us for the tools of language and thought with which we create ideas of order. We are unable to enquire into thought and language without language and thought. It is inevitable that our most original ideas are already given.

Only through the recovery of our very earliest memories can we glimpse a world of light without language and knowledge without understanding.

Understanding is purely personal intensiveness.

How can anyone say anything original? We are weighed down by language and history before we even open our mouths.

'In the beginning was the Word.' It is not until we recover the imperative that we discover how everything came into being.

Thought and language are not contained *in* the world, the world that appears to unfold to our intelligence. Thought and language are super-added to the world. They overlay it. In this way a book is not so much the distillation of things in the world as another object brought into it.

Explanation and meaning are not the same thing. Reasons, as Unamuno says, are only reasons, they are not truths.

Meaning is a subjective hunger for form and order.

Reason must also deliver meaning if we are not to embrace unreason.

We have a post-Darwinian science that knows perfectly well what the mind *must* be, but of course it is the mind itself that must apply itself to the question of the mind, and the mind has its vanity.

The mind has evolved to function integrally with its physical environment, the biological environment it calls itself no less than the extended environment it calls the external world. It is unlikely, therefore, that we can select one attribute of the mind's functionality to stand alone and to say of it that this is *not* an integral function of the mind, but can be made to stand apart from it in order to examine the mind in an objective manner, as though it were *above* the mind.

When we speak of language, we must obey the rules of language. When we think about the mind, we have no choice but to submit to the rules of thinking. We are caught between mirrors.

A rock, we can easily imagine, has no sensation or awareness of anything at all, neither of the world nor of itself. We know that the rock is present to our own sensations. We can imagine to some extent the blankness of the rock outside the scope of our awareness of it. It is not dark, or asleep, or dreaming. It has, in itself, no being despite having, to our eyes, existence. Its absence is so profound that even if we were to bring to it, in our imagination, some sense of its own existence, it would not be sufficient to separate its blankness from the surrounding blankness of the totality of existence. Even to our own minds the spatial and temporal extension of the rock is not clear. A rock, over the course of time, emerges from a larger geological stratum. Where is the rock before it was a rock? On what grounds do we ignore the material from which it has been separated in identifying this matter alone as a rock? If we were to shake it free of the debris of itself in which it now stands, from all the surrounding grains of sand, and say: *This* is now a rock; then we could continue to shake it, across geological time, until there was only sand, and at no point could we *theoretically* arrive at the existence of the rock. The answer, of course, is that only *practically* is it a rock, and that only to the practical mind. The most solid objects in the world are expediencies of mind.

Everything in the world has two natures: its own, which is a complete and incomprehensible blank, an *absence*; or the one it possesses by proxy, imbued with *our* sense of its nature, with *our* awareness of being. And we can conceive of neither one without an act of imagination.

While we can readily admit the blank objectivity of a rock, lost to being in a blank universe, when we start to think along the scale that starts with the rock and works up through the amoeba, plant life, the primitive invertebrate to animals, primates, humans, we grant to them increasing degrees of subjectivity. That is, they are no longer blanks in a blank universe, dependent, as the rock is, on an act of imagination on our part to lend it its existence, but they appear to come into being, grow, act, move, of their own volition. They live, and therefore, for us, their blank objectivity ceases. Yet the same conditions that detain the rock in its blankness pertain to all, the living and the dead, the animate and the inanimate, to ourselves.

If we accumulate sensations through a unique adaptation of our nervous system; if we store sensations as symbolic representations by means of a more effective neural network; if we believe everything we think – then so it is. But we are, none the less, at the deepest level of objectivity, as blank as a rock, a stone, a stick, adrift among the primary materials of a blank universe.

Our lives *are* blanks. What we read in the world is what we ourselves have written.

Objects are features of an *inner* landscape.

In one type of visual agnosia, the phenomenon known as 'blindsight', reported in a number of clinical studies, we have an intimation of the nature of perception in the absence of consciousness. In the agnosic person, as far as the subject is concerned he is completely blind. He can see nothing and he knows that he cannot see, and shares the same sensory deprivation common to the blind. But he can walk across a room avoiding obstacles in his way, in circumstances where he has no familiarity with the room through any other sense data. The part of the brain that is damaged is that area responsible for 'seeing', though the neural pathway from the retina to its receptor is unimpaired. He has sight, but cannot see. This is the right metaphor for the nature of sight in millions of creatures. Extend this phenomenon to all senses, and you have what I mean by the integrity of the objective.

At pre-conscious level, experience is integral, associative and does not require a sense of self.

We can say that, in lower animals, their cognitive and behavioural worlds are integral and objective. The instinctive cognitive world is characterised by the tension and interaction between innate, outer-directed impulses and external signs that release innate patterns of behaviour. There is no question of thought, reflection, consideration, choice. No act is initiated by a decision to act, no idea of self is present in an intuitive act of self-preservation.

An animal's cognitive world is bounded by its own breath, by its own interests.

Acts of self-preservation that are unconscious and reflexive and acts of self-preservation that are conscious and reflective have the same ends. They are both explicable in evolutionary terms.

It would be folly to believe that our own human cognitive architecture, which superimposes a complex conceptual and symbolic structure over a primitive behavioural foundation, now stands entirely instead of all that we have been in the course of our evolution, that there is no longer an underlying dependency on an innate, undetermined, objective and alien self. But precisely because it is alien and unknown to us we have to find metaphors for the self we do not know, the submerged self.

The mind also is a menagerie. It has its zoology, its palaeontology, its Burgess shale, its Cambrian explosion, its unique lost forms of being, its smouldering seams of the Carboniferous.

In many respects our lives are lived for us. At one level our lives are involuntary. Ontologically we have no part in our origins; physiologically no act of volition is required of us in order to breathe. All our lives our bodies are mysteries to us. We dress, shave, comb our hair, we look at ourselves in a mirror. We carry with us a miniature reflection of ourselves, a snapshot in the mind's inside breast pocket. But the body itself is an alien universe with its own rules of behaviour, self-sustaining, containing and limiting our voluntary actions, circumscribing our will, threatening to break down, as it inevitably must, and shipwreck the idea of the self on the void from which it has just now emerged. The reality of the self and its will can be found nowhere else but within the orbit of this involuntary biological entity.

All reality is – is something to get a grip of – the mind acting on behalf of the hand.

The mind grasps the objective, just as the hand does. The evolution of the hand and the brain are intimately involved. Were we able to lay down the mind's objects as we can the hand's, we should also let go of the self, which is one of the mind's objects, we should surrender ourselves to the objective.

The truly integral experience contains neither a subject entity nor an object entity, neither an experiencer nor the experienced, neither an inner perceiver nor the outer perceived. We are unable to understand this from direct experience. The mind has no understanding of an integral experience. What is integral is lost to us, since what we 'know' must stand apart, must be *something*, an artefact of consciousness.

The mind's ideas and the mind's objects are those that the mind regards. The ideas and objects that the mind does not regard are neither ideas nor objects.

The self is an object of perception just as much as a leaf, a tree, a snail or a frog.

I, I suppose, have no mind. But my mind, it supposes, has an I.

Movement first gave rise to perception. Movement stimulated the emergence of the brain itself. Nothing that does not move requires a brain. Neither would it be necessary to have any perception of the outside world if there were no movement in it. Inner and outer movement are the foundations for the neurological structures of all animated life, from which we derive the origins of perception and the construction of reality. The larva of the sea squirt swims around in the ocean. It has a primitive brain. When it settles for life attached to a rock, it consumes its own brain. The brain is functional, utilitarian and disposable. This thought is unpalatable to us, because it implicitly identifies consciousness also as functional and utilitarian. What we seem to ourselves to be, in our innermost being, turns out to be the fiction of an evolutionary mechanism of perception. It is of a greater order of complexity than any other creature's but, none the less, just as fundamental to successful or unsuccessful living as the perceptual functions of the brain of the sea squirt or the pterodactyl.

The origins of the modern mind's ordered perceptual world are to be sought in the common context of the uses of perception.

There is an incipient logical form of order present in the pattern of innate responses to sign stimuli. Similar innate responses to similar external sign stimuli establish a 'class' of external phenomena – but not by virtue of their intrinsic characteristics, rather by the consistency of behavioural responses. A class of predators is actually a class of responses to predators. Order is present only in the order of our perceptions.

Thus we can say that consistent intention = persistent extension.

No object can ever be 'simply' an object. Objects, arising in the mind, are necessarily complex. A tree that might to the instinct of a bird be simply integral to the pattern of its resting or roosting behaviour, when described as a 'green tree in leaf' is already too complex an object to support objective analysis. Much more so is the self. By the time the self has come into existence as an object it is already a conglomeration of physical and physiological things and mental and psychological apprehensions, to the extent that even a preliminary attempt at analysis will lead to the conclusion that the idea of the self as a singularity can only be an illusion. Such singularities are, of course, useful illusions. All objects are illusions compounded of mental possession and mindful intention.

Order has a grammar of order. The grammar of order precedes the grammar of language. The grammar of order creates the preconditions for a grammar of language. A fierce lion running is a unit. It is one thing to the lion and one thing to the antelope. But the grammar of order separates the running from that which runs, creates a category of objects and creates its attributes. The grammar of language creates subjects, adjectives, verbs, objects – a symbolic coherence of parts that at the level of integrity and intuition remain whole. The whole does not cease to be under the weight of a grammatical superstructure. Yet it is only in terms of the grammar of order and the grammar of language that any event can be said to be understood or even said to be experienced.

The grammar of language reflects the grammar of order, the rules under which reality is allowed to be called real. Reality is the statement itself, and the definitive statement is definitive reality. Hence truth becomes locked in language. *Hoc est corpus meum*. But language is approximation, just as reality is merely contingency.

Order is expediency. The reinforcement of action and reaction, as in the gull's warning cry in the presence of the wedge-shaped shadow of its predator, is expediency. Randomness, arbitrary and accidental behaviour do not aid survival. The processes of evolution are formal.

Consciousness may be too broad a definition of the evolutionary distinction between higher and lower forms of perception. The difference is one between segregation and integration, of the substitution of persistent mental objects for innate repetitive patterns of recognition.

Mental events *are* physical events. They only *seem* like mental events because their special quality is to 'seem'. If we accept 'seeing' as an activity of the brain that does not conjure up a 'seer' to make it work, why should we not also accept 'seeming' without introducing the evanescent concept of the 'mind'?

There can be no objects without a mental capacity for objectification.

Movement is integrity itself. The end of integrity is the beginning of everything.

It is the *persistency* of mental phenomena that makes them more than merely utilitarian. They are the schema of things, they are *all* we know.

When the lion, in his integrated cognitive world, sets out at dusk to hunt, he does so out of appetites that trigger his behaviour, and in response to the visual significance of light and dark, to an innate sense of location and direction, to signals of movement and speed, to the scent of vulnerability. His is a perfected skill that optimises temporal conditions. In no respect can we see in this pattern of behaviour its beginnings in a premeditated sketch of a series of actions to be taken and their possible outcomes. Nor can we conceive, afterwards, of a reflection on mistakes made and lessons learned. Integrity is locked into the present. Alternative scenarios require an artifice of mind capable of representing the present and extending experience conceptually to the possibilities of the future. Consciousness not only deconstructs contiguous phenomena into separate, isolated objects or experiences but breaks apart the same continuum into past, present and future. Consciousness creates time as well as things.

To say that free will is an illusion of consciousness is to say no more than that there is such a thing as consciousness.

He who describes a thing is master of the thing he describes. Why else should we pursue knowledge?

If a machine were suddenly one day by a random accident to generate consciousness, then certainly we would have to say that consciousness is an illusion produced by a mere mechanism. But would this fact, that consciousness is the illusion of a functional mechanism, cause us any concern? We will not be dispossessed of our knowledge simply because we know one thing too many.

Things make sense when our perception of them conforms to our perception of what sort of order *makes* sense. Order must satisfy our sense of order. Facts can only make sense as facts when measured against subjective sets for the criteria of order.

There is no reason why aesthetic judgment should not have its foundation in the same range of evolutionary adaptations for expediency as other forms of perceptive judgments. Is the recognition of a fly that will satisfy the appetite of the frog fundamentally any different from any other form of recognition, including the recognition of order that will satisfy our idea of order? If there is a trigger for 'rightness' of judgment among sense experiences, then there must also be an inherent capacity to respond to it that is equal to the subduing of an appetite by its consummation. Just as in hunger or sex, in judgment, too, consummation is all.

Consummation, in eating, sex or recognition, is fundamental biology. If we can identify the behavioural mechanism for apparent judgment or decision making in the stickleback, then we should be prepared to accept that 'recognition' is as much inherited biology as the consummation of the drives of hunger and sex. Tinbergen has described, in the male stickleback, how the reproductive behaviour pattern is triggered by a combination of ambient temperature and a visual stimulus from a 'suitable' territory. Here we have a subjective, aesthetic term – 'suitable' – in an objective, scientific context. What is 'suitable' is, we would say, a matter of subjective judgment. But at the cognitive level of the stickleback such 'judgment' is limited to an instinctive response to the coincidence of multiple sign stimuli received through its senses. It is, none the less, an act of recognition, a trigger point at which, in a sudden behavioural phase change, the unknown condition sought becomes the known condition found.

At pre-conscious level recognition is a mechanical resolution of inner necessity and outer opportunity. But if the mechanism of consummation is so deeply embedded in the most primitive forms of behaviour, then our own judgment, at conscious level, may depend, however etiolated, upon the same fundamental process. We must know, as the stickleback 'knows', when to say yes.

We cannot arrive at an absolute of order. We can only make judgments, and judgments must satisfy some idea of order. We know the rightness and the truth of something in the same way that the stickleback knows he is home.

Since it is only the *form* of understanding that must be satisfied, we often make unequivocal judgments in the absence of all the facts. How do we know when we have all the facts?

In animals, birds and fishes unequivocal judgment (that is, their innate responsiveness to external sign stimuli) can be elicited by dummies, by false data. The data are false, but the judgment is true.

Rationally, judgment is always provisional since, as the criteria for judgment are theoretically indefinitely extensible, the model against which emerging information is to be judged cannot be completed until every piece of information, including information whose existence is not yet known, has contributed to its modification. Judgment in all things, for all creatures, is pragmatic, since order itself is expedient.

Intellectually, fulfilment is found in confirmation, in certainty. Convictions, we say, are arrived at – arrived at, we like to think, by weight of objective evidence. But the point of arrival is an emotional, even a celebratory encounter. If convictions are to be arrived at then there must be a moment of arrival. While it may be hedged around with intellectual justification, the essence of the moment is emotional and aesthetic. To get to yes there must be a match between evidence or experience and the criteria of judgment. That match must be recognised. Recognition triggers an aesthetic sense of resolution and an emotional sense of satisfaction, without which no hunger could ever be satisfied, nor any question answered. A question is an expression of appetite. An answer is its consummation.

Meaning is satisfaction with our perception of order. Since the criteria for order are indefinitely extensible, our level of satisfaction with order will vary with the experience. It is sufficient for us to have learned some elementary arithmetic for numbers to appear to have meaning when they add up. More complex mathematical solutions require more mathematical language in which they can be satisfied. The efficacy of mathematical judgment is a paradigm for the extension of evolutionary utilitarian mechanisms of judgment and discrimination to abstract concepts which will serve our advantage as conscious beings liberated from the integrity of experience. However, the usefulness of meaning when we enter more intractable areas, such as the 'meaning' of life, is less obvious. Moreover, since the ends of meaning are not apparent, we are presented with an urge to understand that will not necessarily result in any useful discovery. We are obliged to consider, therefore, that there may be varieties of meaning whose meaning lies entirely in *having* meaning. That is, meaning is self-sufficient when it successfully triggers the consummation of question and answer, problem and solution, desire and fulfilment. The content of neither the question nor the answer is material. What counts as an answer is the aesthetic resolution of the question.

Since meaning is emotionally or aesthetically derived, no one statement of meaning has more objective certainty than any other. They are rivals for certainty by virtue of degrees of understanding, levels of reasoning and refinement of appreciation. There are no absolute meanings.

Once we liberate ourselves from the domination of a single idea – that meaning is inherent in the external world and therefore discoverable – and elect in its place the plurality of aesthetic judgment, we free ourselves from the anguish of seeking and not finding an absolute of meaning. We become aware of who we truly are and have been since the emergence of conscious discrimination – the author of this world epic, the artist in his studio.

The foundation of consciousness, reason and judgment are to be sought in our evolutionary history. There is nowhere else for them to spring from. But it does not follow that the totality of our thought processes, our ideas and our intellectual behaviour can be linked back simply to an evolutionary strategy for survival. No doubt sexual selection is another evolutionary impetus that favours survival. But to decide to remain celibate and dedicate one's life not to reproduction but to an overwhelming idea of spiritual selfhood contradicts a theory that would try to pin every freedom to an evolutionary necessity. Evolution has brought us to the necessity of thinking, but we are free to think unnecessary thoughts.

The eye creates in the act of seeing. We are artists before we are anything else.

The first paintings are found in the barely accessible unlit depths of Palaeolithic caves. No, the first images illuminated dreams in the dark recesses of the mind, a magical dependency of external reality on imagination.

Meaning is meaningful when it meets the criterion of meaning. The criterion of meaning is aesthetic satisfaction with the perception of order. Meaning is the corroborative process of a closed system – an entelechy. It is useless to enquire outside it – it is mere illusion to think we can, a failure to grasp the meaning of meaning.

Consciousness, in fact, is its own reward. It is the island of the real risen from the unreal, the *realisation* of being.

How can a question framed within consciousness, employing the questioning faculties of conscious reasoning, have its answer outside consciousness, in emptiness?

We are responsible for reality. In one sense we are directly responsible, in so far as reality can only arise out of consciousness, from a conscious awareness that makes things 'real' as opposed to integral with experience as they are for the bat or the cockroach.

In another sense we are aesthetically and, ultimately, morally responsible for reality since it is of our own making and the source of meaning. Reality is an oddly personal perception of the world and the self, entirely irrelevant once we step outside our own heads.

The iconography of belief is the manifestation of an aesthetic. It is not the imperfect form of reason.

Aesthetically, God is a fact but, rationally, merely a false hypothesis.

All acts of creativity are disdainful of mere *explanation*.

One would have to admit not only the pragmatic but the *intrinsic* superiority of particular analytical mental functions in *all* cases to argue that this capacity to see the thinness of things, the nothing-but-skin-and-bones of our beliefs, denotes the end of them, that henceforth we must go gaunt and anxious in this world though the world each day overwhelms all our senses and our reasons, and in fact presents itself to our reasoning *only* because it comes first from the fiery crucible of the imagination.

It is a mistake to try to explain art, except when art substitutes explanations, manifestos, credos, is-it-art debates for art itself –

then art is grateful for reason.

Reality has no ultimate, settled form. It has the appearance of stability at an epochal, historical level; it is contained for a time within the boundaries of a self-referential culture; it is delineated by a symbolic language held in common. What we hold to be the nature of the world and the nature of the self is a matter of collective responsibility to which the individual subscribes. Yet it is only through the individual that it can be realised.

The individual is the artist, the shaper, the maker.

Reality is a playground.

To assert the primacy of the individual vision of reality as the shaper and maker of reality is, one may argue, to sanction the supremacy of an evil vision. The truth is, we are never free from evil, since we are never free from ignorance.

Evil arises not from thinking but from acting.

When we conclude, as we are inclined to when we look back from our position at the end of time, that when men in the past have subordinated their lives to an article of faith, to an ideal of religion, and, in some instances, have sacrificed their lives rather than relinquish that ideal; that, in the light of what we know now (the truth!), they have been mistaken, they have sacrificed and subordinated their lives in vain; then we cancel out, retrospectively, the meaning and value of their lives. Yet their lives, undoubtedly, had meaning and value. In fact, in the act of cancelling their lives, we are not entirely free from envy of them, envy that arises from our idealisation of a life of simple faith and certainty, an idealisation that may bear no relation to the real experience of those who have striven towards faith and certainty. The dismissal of past lives supposes access to a superior and less fallible truth in our present lives. But all such superior comforts depend on our inability to imagine their lives as our own past lives, or to imagine our present become the past subordinated to someone else's present, or that there are no other truths that will supersede ours, or that there is no past truth that in the course of time will not reassert itself as the truth for us also.

Everywhere in evolution you find plurality and abundance, exuberance and redundancy, the swarming of millions of perfectly satisfactory forms. The natural order of things is towards incremental diversity, not consolidation into one unvarying form. There is equally a self-sufficiency in the diversity of ideas, which multiply and contend but are as perfectly satisfactory in their own strange ways as the hedgehog and the angler fish are in theirs. If there is biodiversity, there is psycho-diversity, and there is no permissible convergence of ideas any more than there is of species.

Our aesthetic responsibility for this world of light, imposed upon us by consciousness, is equally our moral responsibility. If I fail to recognise and understand my responsibility, aesthetically, for ideas of order, then I will not understand or accept my moral responsibility for ideas of order. The world, through consciousness, realises itself in me. But I may misunderstand this and come to believe that, on the contrary, I realise myself through the idealisation of the world. The difference between these two ideas is that, in the first, my vision may be infinitely various and without limitation, while the second is of necessity limited, since it is to be brought into being by the rejection of other possibilities. One illumines the world; the other casts a shadow across it.

There is a bond of meaning beyond reason that must not be broken. Equally, we share a dark pact with illusion, from which only reason can rescue us. This is the paradox of the human condition, that we cannot escape the contradictions of the heart and its reasons.

There are really only two forms of morality. One is based on a personal moral understanding, which by habit of thought and action describes the sphere of our moral behaviour. Since, however, it is constructed on a foundation of reason and experience, it may fail us when we are confronted with a matter beyond reason or experience. But, whenever moral understanding is tested, we do at least, by that very understanding, recognise our failure, and hence the ultimate weakness of our moral constitution. The second form of morality is that imposed from above and submitted to from below; that acknowledged on all sides as the rule of constraint; that to be obeyed by those lacking personal moral understanding. We do not, in either case, unknowingly transgress an understanding of moral behaviour. Moral responsibility always lies within our power, but our power may be less than we estimate. Personal moral understanding is not subordinate to unjust laws. The extent to which our moral constitution fails, and the extent to which it succumbs to the power of unjust laws, is the measure of the moral strength of the individual assaulted by external forces greater than his own and betrayed by the temptations of his own interests. But we are never ignorant of what we do.

Men are still animals in an animal kingdom. We are not free from the struggle for personal survival and supremacy over our enemies; from the exercise of power as a demonstration of our superiority; from selfishness; from herd behaviour; or from fear, courage, obedience, rebellion, affection, savagery. We have sublimated some of these animal urges and rages into civilised courtesies and apologies; but we grin like tigers and shit like any other beast.

Most acts of abomination are acts of reason not acts of passion.

Ignorance always has right on its side.

Not our best behaviour, not our greatest sacrifice, not that supreme act of redemption has removed evil or ignorance from the world. Redemption is the redemption of the self and not of the other.

If I am the creator, then I am not the creature. I will act according to the will of the creator and not from the lowly desires of the creature. These are my choices – my supreme fictions or my earthly desires.

Reason is at two removes from the immediate data of consciousness, first by their objective representation, and then by their symbolic interpretation. Reason can be applied to data, but the data are not in themselves reasonable.

How can reason be objective when it sits in one's head just like any other superstition?

Persistence is the great puzzle. It is as though the wish to continue were held at the fundamental level of the cell. In the absence of the idea of the will we can only imagine some series of perpetual reinforcements at every point of contiguity. Why shouldn't every attempt at coherence *fail?* While it is not difficult to conceive of coherence as the accidental outcome of random collisions, it is impossible to conceive of its subsequent persistence as merely fortuitous. Why *should* cells form the habit of replication and not simply exhaust themselves as singularities? Perhaps in some way we are pleased with ourselves from the beginning.

Once we have admitted the aesthetic ground for being we must agree that God exists exactly in the manner we have always imagined Him to exist.

God is not so much the creator of life as the virtue of being.

If you can establish an *imperative* for being – even if this remains at the level of molecular coherence – that is, coherence is a 'law', an inevitability, a *necessity* (of matter) – irrespective of the *origin* of that imperative in accident – then the rest follows (that being is necessary, is sanctioned).

The immaterial is of no interest if questions about it must always be framed in the material.

The material must be accepted as the given since the immaterial cannot be given.

Nothingness is contained within somethingness.

Science shows a world with order but without meaning. But if meaning is shown to be an attribute of imagination, of the functioning of the mind that has an evolutionary reason for being, then science must recognise imagination as the legitimate judge of meaning and cannot deny our supreme fictions on the basis of an array of facts *without* meaning.

It is sufficient for the fox and the pheasant, the dog and the dung beetle, to be what they are. We do not associate anxiety or regret, ideas or ignorance with their lives. The hen fears the fox but does not envy it; nor does it fail any test of the right to existence by having only two legs and not four. If everything that exists is satisfactory in itself, but a man is unsatisfactory to himself, is not content, from what does this dissatisfaction arise? Only from the hunger for meaning, for the order of things by which meaning is defined. We are in fact no less self-contained in our natures than the animal. But our self extends to consciousness, and consciousness demands order. But consciousness contains the whole world, and worlds beyond worlds, so there is no limit to the self or the self's idea of order; nor therefore to what the self may know or love or be grateful for or shape to the shape of the heart's affections.

Meaning is a closed loop of experience, perception, representation and judgment. There is no meaning outside that loop, since, outside, the idea of meaning *has* no meaning.

Order is my idea of order. Meaning is my aesthetic judgment of order. There is nothing to be done about this. The alternative to subjectivity is emptiness. I know nothing that is not of my own invention. I have no other sanction for being but my own acts of celebration.

3

Order is the mind finding itself again in things.

Henri Bergson

Life is for living, not for thinking. Why, then, do I put it off, as though life were a *reward* for thinking?

Ignorance is by no means the *absence* of thought. Ignorance is an active state of mind. Whole lives are dedicated to it.

We produce nothing unless we believe something.

If we know too much to begin with, we never begin.

Can there be such a thing as immediate experience? Immediate sensation, to be sure. But what is *experience* unless we add the element of subjectivity to it, by which time it is already changed? One might just as truthfully say, 'immediate illusion.'

The simple fact of the case is this: the *a priori* representation of cause and effect *matters* – this is how we get around. We are without legs if we are without reason. But none of this is in things, it is in us. Therefore we never cease to seek causes, as pigs continually root out turnips. We turn to meaning and to understanding out of our natures as obsessively as the pig buries its snout in dirt. That is all our knowledge is.

Thoughts and ideas viewed practically and pragmatically as extensions of the individual's instruments of successful existence – fleet-mindedness as a substitute for fleetness of foot – serve no more *in themselves* than the means of perpetuating the individual in his existential condition. When we appeal to existence for meaning, *more of the same* will never serve as an answer. The answer will always lie not in the practical application of ideas to our continuance but in the *incidental* observation of the condition we seek to perpetuate.

Despite all appearances to the contrary, what matters to us in this life is the *inessential*.

For the animal, life is *all* essentials.

The bird in the tree has no need of the idea of a tree, still less of the idea of a tree *under observation*.

So much effort to free oneself from the tyranny of thinking – when one could have remained an idiot from the beginning.

Yet we can't surrender knowledge and the let the self run itself intuitively, as though nature would take care of us. Knowing too much is part of our nature.

There is *something* incorruptible in God's will and *something* corrupt in man's will. But, in surrendering to God's will, can we be sure we are not surrendering to the very last corruption of man's will, his own egotism?

The only souls who are saved from the beginning are those who are artists from the beginning.

To possess that primal innocence and naivety that is *awake* to possibility but knows nothing – that is true knowledge.

Reason modifies our desires but does not substitute for them. First we are moved and then we look to see what moves us. But reason does not move us.

Christ's command was to accept the given. Life was outside the frame of nature, in the infinite extension of himself.

'Consider the lilies.' The subordination of doing and getting to being and knowing.

Once you have got to the point of abandoning the delusion of a *person* inside the skull, the worm in the jumping bean, you can dispose of the mystery of the will. The will is no more the homunculus of the living organism than the self is. The will is the organism itself, the ambulatory individual living organism.

If the world were not, in fact, populated only with our own ideas of it, we would collide from minute to minute with anomalies, perplexed at every moment, bewildered, smothered, torn to pieces as soon as we saw the light of day, a day indistinguishable from night.

If our existence is not a necessity it is at least our *fatality* (as Schopenhauer says.) But what, at bottom, is the difference between necessity and fate? Since we are, we *must* be.

The consolation for us in *never* being able to know the true nature of things directly or immediately (and even indirectly and intermediated) lies precisely in that very fact of never being able to know. For what if that direct and immediate knowledge were (as we suppose it may be) at once the absolute and irremediable negation of matter and of existence, were the immediate apprehension of one who had been cast for all eternity into blank space? Would we not then be finally and forever inconsolable? Our consolation and comfort are to be found only in what we know, and have thereby rescued from oblivion, which is nothing less than the world itself, and ourselves purposefully adrift on the sea of the unknown.

If there were only *one* truth we could never be reconciled to it.

If it is the task of the philosopher to explain life, then that task is only to settle one sort of argument, to resolve a problem arising solely from one particular response to life, and that a singularly obsessive one, that touches not at all on the multitude of other responses to life that neither ask for nor are given any explanation, including those that belong to the teaming, innumerable forms of unconscious life that do not know they live. Philosophical problems are problems of knowledge not problems of life. Knowledge is the late production of nature with an infinite amount of leisure, just as sick people find time for jigsaw puzzles.

Someone has woken us from our natural state of torpor, and has not stopped to explain or apologise. Why should this state of affairs be supportable? Why should we endure this noise and clamour, this burden of responsibility for something never agreed to? One morning K. awoke... and began inexorably his journey towards death.

To live is to lose myself – I mean, to *just* live – is to admit defeat. I would rather do absolutely nothing at all than live.

Given that all phenomena possess the forms of our potential

actions upon them, there are some objects of our perception that never can support our actions, such as the moon and stars or a distant mountain range. They have a merely decorative or contemplative form lacking in utility and remaining mysterious. They are, in essence, beyond our grasp. Utility and mystery are inversely proportionate, as a can of soup stands in relation to a painting. Hence a painting of a can of soup is a very disconcerting object.

Art is something out of reach represented *in absentia* by the material to hand.

Art is the thing itself, not the commentary on some other thing.

Too many poems have the poem as their subject; too much art is about art; and philosophy never once gets up off its arse.

One does not want to go to heaven for fear of finding that, after all, God is just a Jewish interior designer.

We do not really wish to be saved. We only wish to know that we will be saved.

Truths, we admit, are generalisations from particulars. But the truths of history are in the particulars, and the particulars are ignorant of history, and history is ignorant of the particulars.

The individual has a memory that exists in the present only and serves the permanent consciousness of self; just so, the race has a history without which it can have no identity. But what *is* is not *what was*, for what was is transformed into the materials of the present.

The past is not recollection but perception.

I am what I can recall, or I am only the ebb and flow of my desires.

The *continuous* life (through history, from generation to generation) can, perhaps, be seen as one person constantly changing his mind.

What we strive towards, but can scarcely attain, is a state of pure knowing untainted by any purpose or practical end or self interest, the overcoming of life for the sake of that state of knowing that is more than life because there is nothing beyond pure knowing that we could ever conceive of or hope for, and nothing less that we can settle for.

To have sufficient reason to know how to live makes for a reasonable dog's life.

Necessity compels us to be free.

Suppose everything in its natural state, every particle of matter, is equal and opposite, on the point of coming into and going out of existence; that is, indifferent to being or not being, a mutual cancellation, only, in fact, potentiality for being something or being nothing. Then some error of asymmetry, at the beginning, created an imbalance that favoured existence over non-existence where, before, in countless other begun universes non-existence held sway, a perfect equilibrium of neither one thing nor another, neither matter nor not-matter. Perhaps that is what matter is, what existence is, an error of asymmetry, disturbed equilibrium, an imperfection of order that allowed something to assert itself over nothing and thereafter lay down the rule of perpetual strife, of matter against emptiness, being against nothingness, life against death. The most perfect imaginable world has nothing in it.

Nature justifies no hopes.

If you position two food sources, exactly the same, at equal distances from a hungry bear, what will prompt the bear to choose one thing above another? Probably nothing at all. Choice and decision are projections of the observer after the event. Simply because the bear *will* act there must be a consequence to his action, and because only one thing will happen because two things cannot happen simultaneously, there appears in retrospect to have been choice, but there is no reason to suppose choice was implicit in prospect. We do choose, we believe, because we discriminate between things for our advantage. Selection for advantage is perfectly consistent with every other mechanism of evolution. That we perceive our actions as an exercise of free choice may be no less an illusion, the epiphenomenon of cognition, than the illusions of our existence in space and our duration in time. Freedom is the wider sphere of action for necessity. To what extent do we cease to be creatures of necessity by virtue of freedom of choice if, in the end, we do freely what the bear does of necessity?

The sense of my freedom of action takes the form of the separation of that which thinks, considers and decides from that which acts, as though for a time 'I' were the puppet-master and then, immediately, the puppet. But I am one thing, a self-interested organism, a unit of action. My information-gathering biology and neurology – my antennae become my brain – are a tangle of perceptions, narratives, illusions, projections, representations, including the one that convinces me I am the agent of my own will. But I am just that one thing, that flounders towards its destiny, its thoughts flailing the air like the wings of a bird in a storm, like a man drowning.

Why is freedom important? Is the importance of freedom the need to exercise power, is freedom power in another guise?

There are those who fear freedom: they desire only to submit themselves to another power, to someone else's exercise of freedom.

Our happiness lies in endeavours, not successes.

At the point at which Cinderella marries the prince our interest in her ceases. We believe stories set off badly but turn out well in the end, but in fact it is the story itself that engages us and the ending is just the point at which everything to which we have given our attention vanishes.

So here we are, conscious, sentient, reasoning beings *disappointed* with experience.

Where is the radiant perfumed Christ of our hopes but here in our bitter experience?

Truth and death must be one and the same, since after them there is nothing of interest.

Death is a singularity. You don't need to dedicate your life to it.

Death, of course, is an *idea*.

The evolutionary value of the emergence of consciousness is in the creation of the illusion of subject and object, knower and known, observer and observed, the self and its representations, and hence the exercise of power of the subject over its object.

To know is to know neither the content nor the truth of knowledge.

We are as content with error as we are with truth in so much as we are *satisfied* with either.

We should not look for preferment in the natural processes of selection. Survival is not a matter of selection of the better option. Survival is simply a fact of being the remainder of all that in the course of time has failed. Species survive not by exception to the universal rule of destruction but only as a matter of fact in the perspective of time. Are we alone in the universe? Perhaps. It is given to the one intelligent species in the universe to wonder if it is. The concentration camp survivor is singled out as a victim as much as those unnaturally selected for death. He asks, Why me? but receives no answer from his will, only the matter of fact answer of the circumstance.

Non-conformity and originality in the individual have only a small yard in which to exercise. Our subjective selves are invariably proved to be only aspects of collective subjectivity, of language and history. Dissent is always another form of conformity.

Order provides a mask of certainty with which we cover the universe's essential disorder and uncertainty. The more complex and chaotic our experiences, the more we tax the intellectual faculties that impose order on them. The more we understand, the more ordered the world appears to be; the more ordered, the more it reflects our own temperament, which is not only to make sense of disorder but to impose control over it. Understanding is a form of power and a source of authority. An essential form of order for the intellect is language. Through language disparate things, actions, locations, movements, meanings become ordered and coherent; they are supported by the structure of vocabulary, grammar and syntax. Language is the internal confirmation of our authority over phenomena, the articulation of understanding. It follows that those who lack the skills of language have a less ordered view of the world, are less certain, have less control and less power. In reality they do seek to impose order, but within a limited compass. They cling, so to speak, to spars from the wreck of disorder and make of these a universal order, hold fast to limited ideas, received wisdom, narrow perspectives, and seize whatever opportunity for the exercise of power floats past them. The world beyond their horizons remains an enigma, and they themselves are thereby diminished.

The Copernican revolution was a revolution in conceptualisation only. No worlds shifted, only subjective perspectives changed. And far from displacing the subjectivity of the observer at the centre of the universe about whom experience revolves, such advances in the interpretation of phenomena succeeded only in consolidating the role of the subject as the mediator and arbiter of the truth of the observed. If man was the centre of God's universe and the apple of his eye before Copernicus, he is as surely afterwards the gravitational centre of all that might be said about it, and now with the *hubris* of certainty in his judgment that his former self-doubts would not permit him.

Paradoxically, the more we understand empirically and, as we say, objectively, the more centred on the subjective does that objective knowledge become. When once the mythic narratives of experience are discarded and replaced with more complex intellectual schemata then we multiply the intellectual effort required to sustain them. Hence when we fail to make this effort we fall back on simpler and more intuitive forms of understanding. We can never have an objective understanding of the world, only more effective models of its subjective representation. The more rigour required to sustain those models, the more arcane does knowledge appear to be: science becomes one with alchemy, leaving those without the disciplines of understanding to its counterfeit. The subject always determines the rules of reality, and, as in all the games we play, there are rules but not truths.

Just as, in the mind's habitual construction of reality, there is no 'cause' unless an 'effect' is produced, the past does not exist until we observe in the present an event to which a causal history can be ascribed.

There may be an answer to the question of how the universe might have emerged from nothing, but the mind, being something, has no means of accepting it.

Since nothing is meant, nothing is wasted. Everything is equally without purpose, nothing is for the sake of something else.

Experience itself does not question; something else does.

Metaphysical questions do not have empirical answers. The questions must be questioned, the questioner questioned, that is the empirical method, this is where we must look.

A machine will learn to think when it has first learned to shit.

If we say the world is what it seems to be then that world is the work of the mind, for the entire schema of seeming is the mind's work.

The curious longevity of the idea that the true nature of the world is its intelligible nature, rather than the impossibility of such an idea. If our senses deceive us, why shouldn't our thoughts?

Heraclitus: You can't step into the same river twice. But Cratylus: You can't step into a river even once.

Security is to be found only in the smallest personal universes. There is a sort of giddiness that takes hold as we move further away from the centres of comfort – the mother, the blanket, love and other forms of dependency – towards our heliopause, that point in the wider universe where the influence of the sun ends and we float out into space, time and unilluminated matter.

Does the truth require brevity? Perhaps not, but the more we say the more of what we say will be untrue.

There will always be spiritual mass movements, even of the most ignorant kind, in secular societies and states, for no one for long can believe that one's significance *sub specie aeternitatis* will emerge out of mere social organisation for material welfare.

The more we strive the more our actions confirm us in the person we are or have chosen to be, and the prospect of any sort of escape diminishes in exact relation to effort.

Oblivion is my special subject.

All events are mental events. Only after experience, when we have sifted what remains of it, does what actually happened become the impression that takes its place as an event in the mind.

This is what life is: the burden of consciousness, the oppressive weight of memories that are not even ours and the heavy silence of all that we have forgotten.

Ideas don't become less true over time, they simply become exhausted.

One must remember what Rilke says, that suffering is one of our inner seasons.

When the artist measures himself by his reputation – that is, by what is known of him to others – and exchanges what *he* knows for what others know and places that knowledge at the centre of his being, he becomes the regarded object rather than the subject that regards, and he is no longer an artist.

Not to have to argue, to defend, to dispute, but to be private, to internalise – to internalise the earth so that to have lived is to have mattered.

4

The secret of Truth is as follows: there are no facts, there are only stories.

Joao Ubaldo Ribeiro

Reading those ancient arguments of Cicero in his *Tusculan Disputations* for and against the immortality of the soul, the modern mind can't help but think of the burden of belief it has shed by being modern and taking for the foundation of its understanding the natural history of the mind itself. It is something of a relief no longer to have to risk some hidden wrath or retribution for getting hold of the wrong idea about who we are, now that we are largely agreed that we are made of material stuff, and that dreams must be made of the same stuff. But I suppose the shipwrecked might feel the same sense of release, deprived of all possessions, cut off from the acquired habits of civil living and abandoned to their true existential nakedness. We face the choice of saving our souls by remembering who we once were, or becoming simply the creatures of fate, contingency and circumstance.

The soul is now lost from the science of matter and the science of mind. Yet it hovers around, as ethereal as it always has been, waiting to be reintegrated into our theories, not as a matter of fact but as a question of what non-material significance can be abstracted from our material being.

The reductionist argument leads inevitably to the prospect that the mind's final destiny is to preside over its own demise, as 'nothing but' the emanations of brain matter, the nature of whose formal existence provides an amusing party game for philosophers and biologists. Yet it's all too interesting to lead inevitably to despair.

Thought itself resists its own conclusions. It doesn't take much reflection to recognise that it is on illusions, not on realities, that our real lives are built.

Ideas were first the functional propositions of a mind in earnest about its body.

The appearance of the first ideas in their first formulations can hardly have been intended as a means of raising questions about meaning, about the existential meaning of survival to those who managed to survive.

Above all, in evolutionary history, what one has been most successful at is predation: the exercise of power over others, the commission of acts of violence against individuals, the propagation of lies and deceptions for personal advantage and self-aggrandisement.

Thought is not the precondition of action.

We can't escape the fact that we came in possession of consciousness by the same rules of evolutionary adaptation that have left other creatures with their heads down in the depths of unknowing. My existential condition must be exactly the same as theirs, but for the fact of my ability to perceive it. My perceptions are locked into that condition. They don't stand outside it, observing it. So I am only free to the extent that I need to believe that I am.

The early history of the fragmentation of our experience of the world is to be found among the flakes of flint and chipped stone and bone that were both physical and mental objects for the first time.

The instinctual organism and its environment are not two separate things. It is I myself who has lost his original integrity, distinguishing himself by his knowledge of the world and as the subject who knows it.

Without attempting to define what cannot be defined, without saying what consciousness is (as though consciousness had an independent existence and were something more than the experience of knowing) I will say that the point of divergence, between unconscious action within an integrated world of subject and object and the conscious action of the subject on the world as object, signalled the moment at which one world was lost and another found. But the world that was lost was always lost, and remains lost now.

Mind cannot be dismissed as matter. My mind does not think less of itself simply because it now understands that it functions entirely on the basis of permissions given it by activity in the brain. It is always free of its own materiality, and undiminished by deterministic and mechanistic considerations of its origins, for I am distanced from the materiality of my mind by my very understanding of it. Mind is not 'just' something else. It cannot cease to be mind, even though I change my mind about where it came from. Reductionism does not begin a countdown to a diminished form of existence. It can have no consequence for my mind unless I make up my mind to behave mindlessly.

Nothing that is can be diminished simply by understanding its origins.

Consciousness and acts of will are still connected by a tangled thread to their precursors, sensory awareness and acts of instinct. Thinking and understanding have arisen out of the material to hand, not from some abstract stuff brought in from somewhere else. Since it is so, it must be sufficient for it to be so, and I must make myself up from that sufficiency.

Suppose I am a frog. If I am a frog, the identity I have just assumed to myself is denied me. I have no knowledge of myself as an individual, and I have no knowledge of the world in which I live. For my life is an integrated pattern of autonomous behaviour that does not require the idea of a frog. I am not separate from the condition of my existence. I do not know that I will die, because I do not know that I live. My life is this unmediated activity. To be I do not need to know that I am. I gaze out on the world, and never gaze in. I gaze out, half-submerged among pond weeds, but there is no frog that gazes for I know of no such thing. Nor are these reeds, the still surface of the water, the reflections of sunlight, the shadows of the willow, anything at all. How should I represent to myself light or reflection or water or reeds or trees unless I could isolate them from the totality of my immediate perceptions into things with separate existences? But all my experience is one thing containing neither myself nor any external object. I do not know the difference between myself and the world. There are no objects, no tree, no reed, no pond, no sun, no frog. There is nothing at all contained in my world because I do not have the mental capacity to represent the forms of my experience. I cannot represent the forms of things because I have no context of space within which I could represent their forms. Nothing happens, because I have no mental capacity to conceive of time, and therefore nothing has a beginning, nothing continues, nothing exists, and nothing is marked by its absence. And although I have said, 'this can't be because of that,' there is no 'because' for me, for my world without subject or object, without space or time, is a world without cause and effect. It is a world of singularities, of singular events unrelated in space and time, and with no relationship between subject and object. I am all in all at once. These singular events keep recurring but I have no notion of them and no memory of them so that they cannot be said to make up a continuity of experience. If they resemble the cumulative effect of experience, this is because I act in the same way on each occasion. In the absence of the knowledge of space and time, form and causality, in the absence of anything that could be called knowledge, I depend for my existence on the efficiency of my autonomous behaviour, those evolved rules of my being. And in fact my behaviour in this way really is very efficient, since it has evolved over millions of years to fit me to what you humans would call my environment and to the negotiated conditions of my existence. I act in my interests, but I do not know in advance that I will do so. I do not know the consequences of my actions. I do not know any causes for my actions. Even less do I have any thoughts on what things are or why they are the way they are: such leisurely and fantastical pursuits are for humans. Could I have any thoughts on this subject, they would be that some parasite had wormed its way into the human brain during that species' earliest existence and created a delirium of illusions that has upset the natural order of things, which is to know nothing and to act in accordance with the habits of acting engendered in organised systems over aeons of time.

Perhaps, indistinctly, some part of our mind recalls, in its mythology of loss and exile, the lost paradise of unconscious integrity and the exile of the unconscious self to the realm of self-knowledge, of will, of labour and death. Emil Cioran: 'Deep in his heart, man aspires to rejoin the condition he had before consciousness. History is merely the detour he takes to get there.'

In the beginning there were no objects in the world for there was no mind with which to discriminate one thing from another. The dung beetle's object of desire does not need to be an object to be desirable. What it turns its attention to is something, but *what* it is or *that* it is are matters of no consequence.

The eye and the hand led the brain's evolution. To grasp something means to grasp something in the mind in conceptual space as much as to grasp something in the world in its actual location.

Our freedom is not really freedom, but rather an excursion to the outer limits of necessity.

Our freedom must have been made in the same workshop in which all the other bonds of nature have been forged. The mind is the bond of freedom.

Reason is the burden of consciousness. It widens our field of vision beyond the things we need to know, to things that lie outside the perception of the eye and the compass of the hand, to the useless as well as the useful, to things of the imagination that are but are not yet, to the impossible as well as the possible.
If reason began simply as a practical and useful shortcut to behavioural conclusions, in the way that the rudiments of wings developed to regulate body temperature – well, now we have wings, and we fly.

Unwittingly (for it has no wit) nature has not limited our understanding to what is necessary. The interests of futurity can't be determined in advance, the boundary of our mental domain is not fixed, our mind wanders where it will, no one knows what necessity means.

Ideas rattle around in the mind like dried peas in a box and have no bearing on the world except insofar as we determine to make the world bear them.

One of the practical economic constraints of the understanding is that it expects answers to be definitive, and preferably singular.

The mind makes up its own inviolable rules, without the benefit of any evidence in experience: the universe must have had a beginning; a finite universe is inconceivable because we can always think of something existing beyond where we draw the finite line; a first cause must have a prior cause; in mathematics the same calculation will always give the same result; the world must have some underlying unity of substance or principle; the unchanging is more true than the changing.

In Daniil Kharms's story, 'A Sonnet', the writer can't for the life of him remember which comes first, seven or eight. He asks various people. It turns out that everyone can agree on the sequence of numbers from one to six, but beyond that is everywhere a matter of conjecture, opinion or recollection....

Supposing we could discover the 'truth' of matter and mind, why should it turn out to be something that we should be glad to know?

What if we could answer the question, Why does God allow such terrible things to happen in the world? and the answer was simply, Because he was not paying attention at the time, copulating with some other divine being in another universe?

Dostoevsky said in *Crime and Punishment:* 'We always imagine eternity as something beyond our conception, something vast. But why must it be vast? Instead, what if it's one little room, like a closet in the country, black and grimy with spiders in every corner, and that's all eternity is?'

Why would we know more by encountering in reality what we have created in our imaginations? If we could come face to face with Christ in the flesh, what more could the frail frame of this man bear than the history of all that he has already borne?

In reading 'Paradise Lost' I am soon on the side of Eve and her argument for knowledge and experience in defiance of 'Our great Forbidder, safe with all his Spies/ About him.' For this Heaven of Milton's imagining is all amarant and gold and amber, garlanded and inwreathed with flowers, paved with jasper and filled with the sound of hosannas and symphonies that are never more than 'charming' or 'melodious'. Here angels spend their days in 'joy and hymning' – but what have they to be joyful about if they have no experience beyond 'hymning'? As Midas was cursed, so too are our best ideals – everything we turn to becomes gold or pearl, ambrosia and nectar – and if we still have evening and morning in paradise it is not of necessity but for variety, for Milton, too, must have seen the tedium of his own conception and tired of his unreal feast.

There is hope on earth, but there is no hope in heaven.

I don't want my life defined by unknowable singularities, for to do that would be to define my life by the fact of death, that most singular and unknowable of all facts.

I have to solve all my questions out of the sufficiency of my being.

If it is the soul that distinguishes me from all other creatures, and the soul is a fiction, then it is my fictions that distinguish me.

As well as the Kantian categories of the understanding that contain the limits of reason, there are categories of self-revealing and self-concealing narratives that contain all the possibilities of meaning.

Pessoa says: 'To narrate is to create, whilst to live is merely to be lived.' We should not fear for our lives, but for the impoverishment of the stories by which we live.

Science is a narrative of the world where reason is the hero and knowledge itself the sufficiency of a mind bent on knowing.

When the mind can't contain itself within the limits of experience and reflection, it looks for transcendent forms of epic order in the transforming myths of history, the religious mass movements of revelation, in final purposes, promised lands, heavenly fields, second comings, resurrections, transfigurations, apocalyptic judgments and restitutions, and the beautiful idea of redemption.

Great ideas sit in judgment on the poor creatures whose minds gave birth to them.

In our universal epic narratives, what fate awaits sinners, heretics and infidels; what great pit is dug by history for all that history will overrun; what carnage is promised to those mere men who stand in the way of the progress of man.

We are the undetermined creations of our own stories, which have any number of beginnings for which we can never find a suitable ending.

It is through our noble fictions that we justify, in the absence of any absolute necessity for being, our willingness to be.

5

I cannot have a temperament other than my own. Nor an aesthetic other than the one which is the consequence of my temperament.

Gustave Flaubert

How much, for what we consider meaningful in life, we depend on the presence of someone else. How easily we abandon ourselves in order to define our happiness in terms of what others will say or do or be in relation to us.

Lovers are like the drowned, holding hands as they are swept into unfathomable depths. They exist for each other, and signify something that, without each other, would signify nothing.

Are our affections merely temporary refuges, somewhere to hide from the truth, the truth of our essential solitariness?

The questioning mind voyages pointlessly towards a conception of an objective and understandable form of truth, of pure intelligence. But there is no such thing as a disembodied mind capable of thought independent of experience.

Someone else's idea of the truth would be hard to live with, for ever and ever, like being a lodger and forever hearing other people's children on the stairs.

What would I actually do in the light of revealed truth, if all that keeps me going are my own fictions?

There are pluralities of truth because truth is not an absolute but a sufficiency.

We can deny the truth, but we cannot deny the sufficiency of the truth, for we would have to deny our own affections.

All the wisdom of the world tells us to judge ourselves by our own measures, but all our instincts seek our value in the judgment of others.

There is no larger narrative written for us, just the day-to-day stories of our own invention.

There is nothing more important to us than knowing. Nothing exists for us without our knowledge of it. Naturally our own significance lies in an assurance of the reciprocation of that knowledge. We ourselves need to be the object of knowledge – known and loved by someone else, in the first instance, and then by God. We want the universe itself to know we are here. Schopenhauer: 'Deep down in man lies a trust that something apart from him is as aware of him as he is himself; the alternative, vividly imagined alongside infinity, is a terrifying thought.'

I need to count, to someone somewhere. My unhappy delusion is that I can count in absolute and unequivocal terms by finding some measure of certainty in the world that is not simply my own invention.

The failure of reason, said William James, is 'to treat abstract principles as finalities, before which our intellect may come to rest in a state of admiring contemplation.' The intellect does come to rest, over and over again, but the point at which it comes to rest is always in fact the point of contentment with the intellect's own discovery and with what it is prepared to assent to. What the intellectual sources of that contentment might be are entirely dependent on the nature of the expectations to which the intellect's discontent has given rise. If we were never discontent we should never need, like Dorothy, to look farther than our own backyard.

Satisfactions are not finalities, only renewable moments of agreement.

Things are so when I turn my mind to their being so, whereas they are nothing at all outside experience, and may be something else entirely on another occasion as another experience.

Only the constant renewal of my mental experiences affords the necessary illusion of the continuity of experience itself. I do not believe something all of the time. I do not believe something when I am asleep, and I do not believe something when I am distracted by the need to act and not think. I only believe something when I recollect my belief and recall it to my mind or recall myself to it, which had for a time entirely disappeared from view. Where was it all this time?

The continuity of reality is only captured in disconnected momentary experiences, yet we manage not to be disconcerted by the way the universe comes and goes.

The criteria by which we recognise something as being the thing it is must be discontinuous, because some condition or circumstance will have changed from one experience to another. The criteria must therefore relate to the nature of judgment and not to the nature of what is experienced.

Doubt is a condition of faith that constantly needs to be resolved. Theories that have been stable paradigms for generations get revised and discarded. These are the large scale discontinuities in the experience of knowing something.

Experience itself is discontinuous. What is continuous in experience is the regularity and constancy of our acknowledgement of experience. If we were unable to recognise something in experience, that experience would have no content and could not be called an experience at all, but would simply be a flow of sense data without significance. It is where in the flow of experiential data we interrupt it to acknowledge something as being something that determines the fact that something is. If the flow of data were never interrupted by acts of recognition, everything would remain indeterminate, formless, unknown and unknowable. If we never arrested the flow of information at some point, there could never be a point at which we could act on it.

To act, we need to be able to make up our minds from information to hand. We act, therefore, on the basis of what we recognise to be so, irrespective of the possibility that things may be otherwise, that what we know is only provisional, that what we don't know is greater than what we do know, that this is not all the information there is. There are no criteria for truth, there are criteria only for judgment.

The criteria for judgment are prefigured in every form of instinctive behaviour. The nature of desire and the nature of its fulfilment are conjoined at birth, one shaped to the other. In abstract terms, if there were no possibility of an answer there could never be the possibility of a question.

In instinct, organisms demonstrate appetitive behaviour in the form of a desire that seeks its consummation in, and only in, those elements of experience that fit the shape of that desire. If the form of the fulfilment of that desire were not implicit in the desire itself then the desire could never be consummated. The corollary is also true. The criteria of judgment for the satisfaction of a desire could never have arisen in evolution unless the continual exposure to the experience of a successful goal had not established what the criteria must be that would determine the desire. In the judgment the stickleback makes when he decides on a suitable nesting location he does not take account of all the facts, of all extraneous data, of other cognitive information beyond the coincidence of visual signals, temperature, the seasonal release of instinctive patterns of behaviour and, of course, does not and cannot concern himself with anything that is forever outside his experience. The organism forms its judgment solely on the basis of the criteria of judgment, and those criteria are defined by prior expectations, which themselves are defined by prior experience in the course of its evolution, fixed now in the genome.

The moment of judgment is the point of convergence of cognitive data and the preparedness of the organism to act on its recognition. Failure to judge is failure to act.

There can be no quest without the means of knowing when the quest is at an end.

There are uncertainties of judgment because the criteria of judgment are internal concerns not external facts.

A judgment by the organism is only 'wrong' if it results in the modification of behaviour over time through the suppression of mistaken judgments by means of natural selection. It is not intrinsically wrong. It is always intrinsically right, because it conforms to the self-sufficient reciprocity of the criteria of judgment, and there is no other mode of judgment.

The sufficiency of experience is seasonal. It ends, and begins again, like hunger, sex, ambition, understanding. To arrive at one conclusion marks the end of experience.

Organisms that have evolved to react in particular ways to external indicators are often trapped in patterns of behaviour by false external factors that resemble true environmental conditions, in particular where those changed conditions are the result of human intervention too recent to have had any effect on the evolution of behaviour. Asphalt polarises light like the surface water of a pond, so mayflies sometimes lay their eggs on a dry road. Beetles have attempted to mate with discarded beer bottles that reproduce the recognition stimulus of the female beetle carapace. The mating cue for the male Cuban tree frog is the receptive immobility of the female, and males are killed attempting to mate with dead females on the road. The facts of experience need not be true to convince us of their certainty. They need only elicit our assent to them.

We are unable to suspend judgment indefinitely on the grounds that nothing is certain.

We make up our minds in the same way that a frog or a stickleback is prompted to act, by closing down on the stream of data in judgment, by obeying signals for completion, by recognising in the attributes of an answer the conciliation of the question. It is this fact of completion, this point of recognition, this moment of resolution that constitutes 'knowing', and not the sum of all the facts or impressions or information that make up the experience, all of which are able to exist as an uninterrupted flow of sensation without ever becoming something known or apprehended.

No appetite is insatiable, because an appetite is mapped to its satiation. No desire is incapable of being fulfilled, because it is modelled to the shape of its fulfilment. No question is unanswerable, because the nature of an answer is always predicated on the question. In behaviour, a capacity to recognise the point of reconciliation is the prerequisite for action; in knowledge it is the necessary ground of knowing.

It is the sense of satisfaction, of something having been concluded, that characterises the nature of a solution. There is no intrinsic difference between truth and error except our willingness to accept one in preference to the other.

That other people hold beliefs that to me are untenable is evidence that every truth is an assent to some sufficiency of information that is only ever partial, and might at another time be something else. The test of truth is our satisfaction with it. We cut up the cognitive world into patterns that satisfy our need that it should have some pattern or order in it. We are like children who fold sheets of paper and cut out one thing that opens out into multiplied replications of what they have cut out just once. Sometimes they are stars, sometimes they are lines of joined up figures dancing, and we are pleased with one or we are pleased with the other.

6

I am certain of nothing but of the holiness of the heart's affections.

John Keats

Reason cannot guide us to certainty, objectivity or truth. It can only help us discriminate between judgments that do not conform to the rules of reason, the irrational, and those that obey the principles of the sufficiency of reason and are therefore rational or reasonable or, as we prefer to say, for all practical purposes and empirical judgments, true.

What is certain, objective or true is so solely by virtue of its conformity to the rules of reason for what is certain, objective, true.

To form the judgment that 'this' and not 'that' is true we must be able to recognise the conformity of 'this' with the rules for 'this' being true, and to know that 'that' is anomalous and does not conform to the rules for 'that' being true. Where the rules come from is lost in the primeval swamp of our origins, but there are no further grounds on which the rules of conformity can be judged.

Everything in its natural state is anomalous. I am unable to comprehend anything that happens in even one second of time without excluding almost everything that did happen and suspending belief in the objective existence of time. For in that second a bird flew overhead, a drop of rain fell on a window pane, and millions of others fell elsewhere, a bluebottle buzzed in a kitchen in Arkansas and a fly landed on a cow in a village in Zambia, and on and on without end. In that one second of time nothing, nothing at all, not for one person or for one thing or for a single atom of matter, is the same thing, but all is anomalous chaotic swarming. Only our attention creates order, by selecting from experience what we will give attention to, and by securing the location of those things in time and space, and ascribing existence to them and setting their existence on the grounds of causes for their being thus, and agreeing with our reason that they are something and not nothing, and one thing and not another. And whatever those things are, the important point is they are no longer anomalous. They remain anomalous in themselves, but in our knowledge of them they cannot remain anomalous and also be known. For knowledge of things is knowledge of the order of things and not of things as they are in themselves.

When we say we understand something, we mean that it is no longer anomalous (it is not understood if it is anomalous) but makes sense (it is understood when it conforms to rules of order). It is understood when it conforms to the *a priori* principles of the understanding, for that is what understanding is. And it is known to be understood when we recognise its conformance. Knowledge is the recognition of order, and that there shall be order is the *a priori* condition of the possibility of understanding.

The beauty of understanding is in its efficiency. How easily it disentangles the shapes of reason from the tangle of intertwined phenomena. How determinedly it disposes of the inconsistent and the erratic, the amorphous and the undefined. How skilfully it retrieves a triangle from all the figures of earth and air. The beauty of instinct, too, is in its efficiency. How the crow knows the branch will support it and not this twig. How the sparrow knows the twig differently. How each will coordinate its movements to conform to the adequacy of what it knows.

Things are true when they are efficient, when they suffice. This is the pragmatic definition of truth. Truth is what works, what serves, what does not fail us. As for the truth of idealism – a carpenter will say a thing is true when it does not veer from its perfect measure, from the horizontal, from the perpendicular. It is true if it has no imperfections, if it conforms to our idea of its perfection. It is not true if it retains vestiges of the anomaly of phenomena not relevant to our idea of its perfection. To be true is to be constant and unvarying. But this is not a permissible definition of the truth of things in themselves, only of the habit of the understanding in seeking the form of stability and order in its ideas of the world.

A theory is true if it fits all cases. It is anomalous, imperfect, untrue if does not, even by one single instance of exception. Yet how can all cases be accommodated to a theory unless the theory determined at the outset to be the perfect form of the accommodation of each case?

The judgment of truth is not pronounced on anomalous phenomena. The judgment of truth is pronounced only when, as the glove fits the hand, what is to be understood conforms to the understanding's idea of what the form of understanding is. The understanding remains restless for as long as it fails to recognise in any phenomenon the form of its understanding. It is dissatisfied until experience conforms to the expectation that will satisfy it. It is satisfied only at the moment of recognition of conformance. This conformance can have no connection whatsoever with any absolute value standing outside the understanding, that might exist outside the sufficiency of meaning contained in the understanding's assent to the form of its understanding.

All judgments are aesthetic judgments. They are satisfactions with the forms of understanding and not absolute judgments of things themselves. The understanding is a self-sufficient, self-contained, self-sustaining system of aesthetic judgments that admits of no absolute measures of judgment external to it. The intellect will finally come to rest when it is able to shift its attention from the irritable obsession with truths outside itself, and come to terms with the aesthetic sufficiency of its own judgments.

Keats's idea that beauty is truth and truth beauty – and not only that we might equate the two but that the conformance of one with the other is all we know and all we need to know on earth – is the epitome of the principle of aesthetic sufficiency. We know nothing, understand nothing, make sense of nothing unless we translate the incoherence of immediate experience and the incomprehensibility of disparate phenomena into the forms of order that are the forms of the understanding. Until we put things in order, all is disorder. Until we recognise order, we do not know the ends of our ordering. In natural history the ends of order are the efficient and economic means of furthering the continuance of the organism. Those means may not be intrinsically 'beautiful' in any commonly received sense of what distinguishes the beautiful from the ugly. But the scorpion and the hippopotamus and the hideous monsters of deep seas without light have their adaptive beauty as much as the nightingale and the butterfly. They are the apotheosis of everything they might have been by being what they are. By being the true representations of themselves they possess the beauty of their sufficiency. For the reasoning mind, the ends of order are equally the efficient and economic means of continued existence. As evolution has eliminated inefficient activity, undirected behaviour and unwise decision making, so it has consolidated the lessons of successful actions into mental schemata of discrimination, selection, judgment and choice of actions. The dog will bite and the scorpion sting and the male stickleback attack its intrusive rival when the conditions of their potential actions are equal to the conditions of actions that over evolutionary time have proved themselves the general guarantee of survival. In the same manner and for the same reasons, the conscious human brain will make up its mind when the conditions of its need to do so match the modes of apprehension that have proved to be the means of its own success. In all cases, whether as instinctive consummation or mental comprehension, the moment of truth is the moment of recognition of what will serve the case, and only order will serve. Keats: 'Thought in action has for its only possible motive the attainment of thought at rest.'

That the aesthetic judgment of order alone might constitute the sufficiency of experience was suggested by the twenty-two year old Keats in a letter, that famous letter in which he wrote of 'Negative Capability' thereby bequeathing to the world two imprecise words for an imprecise idea that has had a life of its own ever since. He was making some comments on Shakespeare, and that distinguishing quality of Shakespeare which is the absence of Shakespeare himself upon his own stage, the absence of his opinions, point of view, philosophy. Shakespeare mirrors our actions, follies, doubts and certainties, while having himself that capability to be without certainty, without a comprehensive explanatory programme 'when a man is capable of being in uncertainties, mysteries, doubts, without any irritable reaching after fact and reason.' But Keats was also thinking of Coleridge, 'incapable of remaining content with half knowledge.' For it is this irritability and discontent of the intellect that seeks its resolution and satisfaction in more certain schemes of order, unable to accept phenomena as they are, discontent with the sufficiency of experience: 'What a happy thing it would be if we could settle our thoughts, make our minds up on any matter in five Minutes and remain content – that is to build a sort of mental Cottage of feelings quiet and pleasant – and to have a sort of Philosophical Back Garden, and cheerful holiday-keeping front one – but Alas! this never can be – .... the spiritual Cottager has knowledge of the terra semi incognita of things unearthly; and cannot for his Life keep in the check rein – or I should stop here quiet and comfortable in my theory of Nettles.'

We can measure our lives in degrees of contentment and degrees of acceptance of what Wallace Stevens has called 'the rhapsody of things as they are' and, alternatively, in degrees of discontent, restlessness and irritability.

Ideally, the sufficiency of order would be found in the comprehension of all things. That is a power we invest in God, the knowing of everything-at-once. Our own knowing is partial, from moment to moment. But if we can extend the moment, as Bergson illustrated the extension of time by extending the duration of this sentence...., then we may also extend the limits of our judgments by accepting more and more anomalous phenomena into the tangled nettles of experience, refusing to close down in judgment, rejecting all theories, accepting contradictions, living with inconsistency, acting without understanding – intoxicated with the impressions of the senses we resist making sense of.

The mind inexorably seeks order. It does not revel for long in its own disorder. There are both limits to reason and ends to chaos.

We must learn to accommodate our minds to the reality of infinite degrees of order, multiple levels of understanding and pluralities of meaning, all of which are aesthetically sufficient in themselves.

There can never be anything that resembles a universal sufficiency of order. Our satisfactions are too dependent on either the character we are given or on experience itself. In fact, we must admit that the only source of judgment of what constitutes the sufficiency of order are those innate propensities and dispositions of temperament and character, hardened into the verities of experience. The origins of the one are to be found in the genetic and physiological construction of the person, but the sources of the other must be looked for in the earliest experiences that will form the neurological fixities of the personality.

Schopenhauer regarded character as innate and immutable, the seedfall inheritance of the father's wilfulness modified by the receptive qualities of the mother. He quotes Propertius: *Naturae sequitur semina quisque suae* – 'each is guided by the talents with which nature has endowed him.'

Current research illuminates the extent to which character and behaviour are predisposed from birth, even from before birth, to be what they will become. Characteristics such as self-confidence, sociability, timidity, irritability, some sexual preferences and suicidal inclinations are either inherited dispositions or the contingencies of being born as a particular lump of flesh and bone. Oxygen deprivation in embryo, premature birth, physical fragility: if he is fragile at birth and grows up sensitive to cold may he not also grow to be circumspect of risk, disdainful of overt competition and maybe measure the value of his sensitivity by his sensations alone? Perhaps by attempting and failing to overcome his weaknesses he may come to think of himself as a failure in other respects. If he is short in stature will he not try to find compensatory strategies for social success that seems statistically to accrue to those who are tall simply by virtue of being tall? We do not make ourselves. We strive with ourselves, and our striving confirms us in who we are.

The condition of being born is the condition of potentiality of experience. The given and largely unalterable physiology of body and brain will engender variability of experience and consequent variation in the construction of the realities of the world and the self. But this is to say no more than all that is uniquely fabricated is in some small way imperfect and unlike its idealised shape, just as a pot or a musical instrument retains its individuality and in fact has its aesthetic value in its integrity as a unique object and not in its conformity to a perfect model.

The subtle limitations of mind and body that might expand in experience to distinct personalities are less the causes of the distinction than the ground or condition on which the distinction will gradually be constructed.

In order to recognise the importance of the principle of aesthetic sufficiency as the arbiter of meaning it is not necessary to understand or concern oneself with all the manifestations of the individual that are or might be consequent on either physical capacities or mental capabilities, or to take account of every formative encounter and experience. It is only necessary to try to isolate among them those manifestations that will decide the criteria of judgment on which distinct sufficiencies of meaning will be founded in the individual consciousness.

The obscure sources of our sufficiencies are forever lost or indistinct. They cannot be recalled because they belong to the mind's period of formation of which there can be no residual traces, for such traces that we might imagine to exist have evolved into the memories and impressions that we do recall – and into memories and impressions reinforced by their recollection and retelling – the origins of which are overwritten for all time. Nor can we compensate by experimental observation for not being able to remember or experience again those first formative mental exchanges in the brain that are to become the maps of our thoughts and our memories. Whatever we observe at any instant, whether in noting behaviour or response to a stimulus, or by imaging the activity of neural networks, we cannot see in all the varied patterns of neural firing anything that might ultimately constitute an experience, any more than we might observe in blown grains of sand the predictors of the moving shapes of desert sand dunes.

Who can say which of the millions upon millions of micro-exposures to circumstances will shape our fears, uncertainties and insecurities, or where exactly we might pick up the thread of the narrative of our being that will be for us the surest line to follow through those same uncertainties and fears? It is impossible to conceive that out of the accidents of experience and the contingency of uniquely prescribed physiochemical capacities of brain and body there emerge minds so alike in form that subsequent judgments made by the mind of one life will share with another life the self-same uniform mould in which those judgments were formed. That the mind will and must judge, reason and form an understanding, is given in the evolved nature of the mind as the body's instrument of judging, reasoning and understanding. But the criteria by which it shall judge are not given as absolutes but as infinitely variable measures of the certainties of experience formed uniquely in the individual mind.

If the measures of experience are uniquely variant, they are none the less equal in status, equally valid, in that they are the necessary measures for proceeding in life, measures of the adequacy of the thread we have picked up as our lifeline. Our doubts may be absolute, certainties never can be.

Since we cannot speculate on the unknown and irretrievable primal sources for the origin of the aesthetic sufficiency of experience we must seek those sources among the things that we can recall, knowing that they are built on even earlier foundations. They begin with the earliest forms of comfort, reassurance and certainty. The infant is not pacified by explanations of causes and probabilities. No reassurance has more power than reassurance itself. My primal comforts and certainties are derived from the degrees of responsiveness to my cries and discomforts, and the answers to my distress lie in the affections shown me. These are the things to which we cling, and we are lost and abandoned without them, as later we may cling to other assurances without which we are lost. From such beginnings do we mingle Schopenhauer's 'small fear of the abandoned child and the "great" fear of metaphysical homelessness,' and learn to seek in the representation of the world and the self the further representation of our deepest desires in the form of our first affections.

Our first affections are our only certainties. It does not occur to us, as infants and children, that the aura of meaningful existence that surrounds us is a mere relative dependency on the mother or the father that shields us and defends us from the wider perception of our metaphysical insecurity; or that the mother and the father in their turn may have no other resource for their own metaphysical comfort than the child's reciprocated affection.

By tracing our sufficiencies and certainties to our earliest affections, we recognise that all the other constructions of meaning and the narrative threads of our meaningful or purposeful lives are not derived from any objective or absolute measure of their truth, of which we have no experience, but from the sufficiency of experience itself.

Our primal consolations, that we will later invest in ideas and ideals and the larger certainties of belief, do not desert us – they are evident in the soldier wounded in battle who cries out for his mother, in Jonathan Swift's scribbled note in the margin of his account book on learning of his mother's death: 'I have lost my barrier between myself and death', in Pessoa's realisation that his entire sensibility is rooted beyond his powers of recollection: 'If there is anything harsh or disjointed about my sensibility, it has its roots in that absence of warmth and in a vain nostalgia for kisses I cannot even recall. I am a fraud. I have always awoken on other breasts, warmed only obliquely. Ah, it's the longing for the other person I could have been that unsettles and troubles me.'

Ruskin, writing of the boyhood of Turner, says that 'he attaches himself with the faithfullest child-love to everything that bears an image of the place he was born in... Dead brick walls, blank square windows, old clothes.... You will find these tolerations and affections guiding or sustaining him to the last hour of his life...'

There can be no sufficiency of meaning that exists of itself independently of the sufficiency of its experience, that is, of its aesthetic sufficiency in experience.

We should give it up, this quest for a chimera of the imagination, the idea of truth and meaning, whose origin lies in our larger metaphysical insecurity, and seek answers where they truly lie, not laid out somewhere to await our discovery, but among our own inventions. Our questions, after all, are of our own invention, so why would their answers lie anywhere else but in our innate capacity to create them?

To walk out, to see the earth and sky, to follow the lane from here to some other place I can imagine, to observe the order in the universe imposed upon it in the act of understanding it, to know and not to be some other unknowing thing, to see and not to be unseeing, to be the heir of the world and not merely the floating debris of the inchoate matter of the world, to be the order of matter that knows itself and its order – this is my privilege, the privilege of being human. But what we know and how we know it are the aesthetic prerogatives of the individual, and to discover the sufficiency of life in the sufficiency of experience is the fulfilment of life. We cannot find the consolation for being and then ceasing to be in the indifference of the universe or among things we can never know. We cannot uncover an absolute of meaning. We can only create islands of integrity that are sufficient to themselves, build a house for ourselves by creating order out of disorder, and look for familiar roads until we recognise the one that takes us home. Like Kris Kelvin in the final image of Tarkovsky's film 'Solaris', we each create a world modelled to our consciousness of it and our affections for it in a universe not only without meaning but without the possibility of meaning.

A Priori: An Unscientific Postscript

*It is not that by our sensibility we cannot know the nature of
things in themselves in any save a confused fashion; we do not
apprehend them in any fashion whatsoever. If our subjective
constitution be removed, the represented object, with the qualities
which sensible intuition bestows upon it, is nowhere to be found,
and cannot possibly be found. For it is this subjective constitution
which determines its form as appearance.* Immanuel Kant, *Critique
of Pure Reason*

*In fact, we are justified in asserting that the whole of the
objective world, so boundless in space, so infinite in time, so
unfathomable in its perfection, is really only a certain movement
or affection of the pulpy mass in the skull.* Arthur Schopenhauer,
The World as Will and Representation

To be clear: what is meant by *a priori* are the principles of
the understanding given simply by Kant in the introduction
to his *Critique of Pure Reason*, and defined equally clearly by
Schopenhauer in his early book *On the Fourfold Root of the
Principle of Sufficient Reason*, namely

> knowledge that is independent of experience and even of
> all impressions of the senses. Such knowledge is entitled *a
> priori*, and distinguished from the *empirical*, which has its
> sources *a posteriori*, that is, in experience.[i]

and

a knowledge that determines and fixes *prior* to all experience everything possible in all experience.[ii]

The *a priori* conditions of the possibility of the understanding are given once and for all by Kant as the pure *a priori* intuitions of *space* and *time* and in his discussions of the four categories of the pure concepts of the understanding, which are *quantity, quality, relation* and *modality*.

These are not technical matters of abstruse philosophy. They are the indispensable givens of the mind in nature, without which we are incapable of understanding either mind or nature. They are therefore matters of the highest importance, not only as the fact of the source of an ordered and understandable world of experience, but as the means of clarifying our understanding of understanding itself. We need not here persevere with extracting all that might be gained from a study of all that has gone before. But it is too bad if someone thinks still that the world 'walks into the head,' as Schopenhauer designated the idea, still thinks of the world as one ready made for our perception and understanding, and presenting itself in such a manner that by diligent application we can know it exactly as it is quite objectively without any construction of the understanding being imposed on it. Too bad, also, if we choose to believe that the mind stands apart from animal evolution and can therefore stand above and beyond the facts of the matter as the independent judge of the facts of the matter. Too bad if we insist on holding on to the vestiges of belief in our dependency on the external for verification, explanations, meaning and purpose. Too bad if we hope for a final revelatory intervention in lives that, all in all, are dependent only on living and are totally circumscribed by experience on one side and the representation of reality on the other.

By way of introduction or anticipation we need only say that there are two stems of human knowledge, namely, *sensibility* and *understanding*, which perhaps spring from a common, but to us unknown, root.[iii]

That root is not entirely unknown or unknowable, though the impossibility of completely uncovering it is bound to make slaves to it of thousands of industrious workers in laboratories and departments of philosophy.

What is most needed is new ideas. For every man who has one of them one may find a hundred who are willing to drudge patiently at some unimportant experiment.[iv]

It may be enough, to begin with, merely to sketch out the broad possibilities speculatively, enough to suggest not so much what that common root exactly and scientifically might be, but only to establish that there are roots, that there is sufficient common ground to pre-mental forms of cognition and the mind's intuitive forms of the understanding, to warrant the suggestion.

If we take Kant's concepts and categories as the given ground of understanding, given *a priori* as artefacts of the mind and its rational mental processes, we are left with the unanswered question of how the *a priori* principles of the understanding came to be given, how they got into the mind in the first place. They cannot be regarded as mere abstract principles of thinking created by thinking itself, or as principles of thought arising directly from experience or from thinking about experience. They are not themselves thoughts, but the ground of thinking; not reasons, but the ground of reason. Once we are able to see clearly enough the outlines of those same *a priori* concepts and categories manifest in one or more primitive modes of cognition, we need not then doubt the possibility that the evolution of one into the other might ultimately be traced by following a course that begins in primitive instinctive behavioural nervous responses, and continues through to the development of the brain and the emergence of a consciousness with the marks of its unpromising beginnings still imprinted on it.

It is worth a foray into this tangled and disputed territory, for one must also attempt to sketch out the future shape of all our speculations, that must henceforth take as their premise the materiality of mind and its origins in natural selection. From which, in contrast, it follows that our future speculations cannot give any regard to the alternative idea of the origin of mind and its nature by unnatural election, independent of its own nature. All our attention must be given to mind itself, as the creator and arbiter of all that can be understood. The mind itself, and the evolutionary cognates of its bodily frame, is the source from which all our desires and all our knowledge proceed and the sole judge and high priest and interpreter of what will suffice to be the acme of all that we might desire or desire to know.

In order to simplify this sketch our principle at the outset is that everything that is has emerged from prior states of being; that all observable features of human existence, behaviour and thought have their antecedent forms. Further, we proceed from this premise – that what is given in intuition is the secondary extended representation of what is first given in instinct. That is to say, the conscious state of mind is the second order representation of things that can be given in perception, for all intents and purposes, without representation. We can be afraid of a fierce dog in instinct without having to represent the dog or its state of fierceness, or to anticipate its potential actions conceptually. The translation of one into the other, of the patterns of instinct into the forms of intuition, of the perception of an actuality into a representation of it in appearance, is the principle by which we understand this evolutionary development to have been accomplished. We need not understand, point by point, the exact equivalence of one action or perception in instinct with its subsequent representation in intuition. We need understand only the general principle of the common root of both sufficiently to portray the understanding of mind as the natural development of the instinctive behaviour of organisms with brains but without minds. We may say this just as we may say that the translation of one language into another is perfectly possible without we first learn the equivalence of every word in every language, including languages dead and lost beyond recovery. Equally we can say that undoubtedly between one language and another something is lost in translation and something added, and that language may itself define the extent of our understanding. Further, it is logical and reasonable to say that language as a human faculty must itself have its antecedent forms. Language, which separates out subjects, verbs, objects could not have arisen unless, in our second order awareness of the world, we had first separated out things that act and things that are acted upon from the unity of action. Things must exist in our minds before we give them names, and the grammar of language must have its precedent in the grammar of perception. We may never discover the correlates in the brain for the synthetic assembly of the objects of perception with the language of their representation, but none the less the one faculty exists only because the other exists.

SPACE

Space is not a discursive or, as we say, general concept of relations of things in general, but a pure intuition. Immanuel Kant, *Critique of Pure Reason*

Space and time are given by Kant as the two pure forms of sensible intuition, 'serving as principles of *a priori* knowledge.'

Space is a necessary *a priori* representation, which underlies all outer intuitions. We can never represent to ourselves the absence of space, though we can quite well think of it as empty of objects. It must therefore be regarded as the condition of the possibility of appearances...[v]

The second order representation of objects requires the intuition of space as the condition of the possibility of their representation. It is a fundamental attribute of mind as the condition of the possibility of all appearances, but it is not a fundamental condition of appearances in any other pre-conscious, non-mental modes of cognition in organisms. The frog does not represent the fly as an object of its attention in space, it simply responds to the presence of the fly at optimal distances from its location as potential prey. While both the frog and the fly exist as real objects in the world, they do not exist for each other as mental objects. They are not represented in space so space does not exist as the condition of their representation. However, the potentiality in instinct for the representation of spatial relations in intuition exists in the two forms of relation in instinct. One is the *orientation* of the subject in the direction of its object, which we may call the potentiality of the representation of the subject or self in space. The other is the *location* of an object as the object of attention or direction in relation to the subject, which we may call the potentiality of the representation of the object or other. Since all these relations are given purely in instinct in behaviour the condition of space as the condition of all appearances in perception is not given and there is no need for it to be given. But as soon as we wish to translate what is given in instinct into what must be given *a priori* in intuition, we see that those instincts, which are themselves given, so to speak, *a priori* as the condition of action, require the condition of space as the condition of the representation of both subject and object. The spatial relations given *potentially* in instinct as orientation of the subject and location of the object are given *in fact* in intuition as the ground of our understanding of the existence of objects and their relation to us in their second order representation. To be clear, space is not the precondition of the existence of objects in experience, only the precondition of their representation as objects. The frog gets on well enough without.

TIME

Appearances may, one and all, vanish; but time, as the universal condition of their possibility, cannot itself be removed. Immanuel Kant, *Critique of Pure Reason*

How did time get into the head, as the *a priori* condition of the possibility of the representation of things, without which we cannot conceive of their existence or their absence, their coming into being, their duration, their disappearance? In instinct there is no need of the representation of time *a priori* as the condition of action in time. But, as with space, the potential forms of the representation of the temporal relations of subject and object in intuition exist in instinct. Again, they are twofold. The potentiality for the representation of the subject or self in time is given in the organism's own *lifecycle*. It comes into being, endures, and ceases to be; but, moreover, its lifecycle and behavioural cycle are related to seasonal and diurnal changes, the movement of the earth around the sun, the sequence of night and day, so that the passage of time, as we conceive it, is, as it were, built into the nature of the organism as the condition of its existence.

> The deer on pine mountain,
> Where there are no falling leaves,
> Knows the coming of autumn
> Only by the sound of his own voice.[vi]

But it has no knowledge of time, since nothing needs to be represented, either in space or in time, in order for the organism to pursue its instinctive course in time and space. The temporal cycle of the organism creates the condition of the potentiality for action in appetite, which is one dynamic of its behaviour, that which comes from within as motivation for action. Its other behavioural dynamics come from without, from external stimuli whose condition is change and *motion*. If the organism did not itself change or move, and if there were no movement or change in its perceptual world, then the organism would have no need of perception at all. We would need no knowledge of the world if the world were static, unchanging and without movement in it. Certainly the brain could not have developed into its primary role as mediator of the body's own movements, let alone into the apparatus of perception and conception it later became. We know, for example, of the sea squirt. The larva of the sea squirt swims around in the ocean. Like many other primitive organisms it sports a primitive brain. It needs its brain to cope with its own motion. When, however, it settles for life attached to a rock, it consumes its brain. The brain is functional, utilitarian and expendable once it has managed the change from swimmer to squirt.

Change and movement do not require the precondition of the existence of time in order for the organism to respond to change and movement and to pursue the progress of its own existence in time. But in order to represent to ourselves both change and continuity over time, to represent ourselves as subjects in duration and to represent objects as coexisting extensions in space, we need also to be able to represent both subject and object in time as the *a priori* condition of their existence and their relation. Thus what suffices as temporal appetites and responses to change and movement in instinct, is translated into a sufficiency in consciousness as the intuition of time as the *a priori* condition of the possibility of things existing and enduring, changing and moving. To be clear, the temporal patterns of instinctive behaviour may unfold without the need for the existence of time over which they unfold, but the understanding requires, *a priori*, the condition of time as the necessary condition of the representation of things in perception and appearance.

THE TABLE OF CATEGORIES

For these functions specify the understanding completely, and yield an exhaustive inventory of its powers. Immanuel Kant, *Critique of Pure Reason*

QUANTITY

metaphorically it can be pointed at with the finger, and needn't be broken into a number of sections. Seneca, *Letters (71)*

Within the category of *Quantity* Kant enumerated three concepts: unity, plurality, totality. That is to say, the understanding is able to make separate judgments of objects in appearance as singular objects, multiple objects and as the totality of singular or multiple objects in appearance. The possibility of these judgments can be seen to arise in intuition from their seeming impossibility in instinct. Although we can observe different patterns of behaviour in organisms towards single and multiple entities we should not be misled by this into thinking that the animal makes some judgmental discrimination between single and plural objects, but rather simply that there are different patterns of behaviour that have been acquired over time towards different conditions, without those conditions necessarily being differentiated by any mediatory act of judgment. Birds, fishes, insects may exhibit differentiated behaviour towards single and multiple objects, but they do not count. The perception of quantity as such is a very sophisticated mental development belonging to the higher primates. Before this development, and underlying the possibility of the *a priori* perception of quantity in reason, is the prerequisite antecedent condition of the separation of a singular object from its surroundings, and the discrimination of an object in motion or action from the totality of the object of experience as action. In other words, experiences in instinct are integral experiences containing neither singularities, pluralities nor totalities but only differentiated behaviour towards different experiences. Certainly the animal has its objects of attention and its objects of desire, but they do not exist in instinct in space and time as objects, they exist only integrally as objects with the experience of the direction of an inner desire and its resolution. The existence of the perceived forms of things as external realities, as things in themselves, independently of our potential actions upon them, is irrelevant. Only in intuition is the possibility of the independent existence of the objects of our attention a condition of their representation in appearance. The point of differentiating singular objects at this juncture in our evolution is that we should be able to get our heads around them. If we are to grasp them with the hand, then we must be able to grasp them mentally in representation in appearance. If we are to pursue them as objects of our attention and interest, and as the rewards of the direction of our desire, then they are best set apart from all that is not the object of our desire or attention. They are set apart in instinct, but only as forms of directed behaviour. They are set apart in intuition as representations in appearance for the same ends of directed action or attention (which is no more than potential action).

In perception, what was once whole, and irrevocably whole, is broken apart and, once broken apart, is irrevocably isolated from that whole with which it was formerly integrated. Thus the *a priori* judgment of quantity gets into our head in this way – first we separate out from experience the singularity that is the object of our attention in instinct so that it stands as a singularity in intuition and exists as an object of extension in space and duration in time. But it always had the potential to be an object since it was both the object of attention arising out of instinctive appetites and interests, and the object that would be recognised as the fulfilment of an appetite or interest. Rather than simply that our command of the objects of our attention should be left to find its own ground of instinct through trial and error over evolutionary time, we command them by setting them up as singular objects of the understanding. Once so established in their rightful domain, they can never revert to their original condition of instinctive integration without they become at once unknown and unknowable as objects, for knowledge is knowledge of the existence of things in their representation and not as they are, which is unknowable. To be clear, once we have set the condition of the existence of something as a singularity, we have no other way of perceiving things except as pluralities of themselves, and no way of perceiving the whole except by adding together those pluralities into a notion of their totality. But their totality is beyond our experience, for it is an artificial, synthetic representation of the whole we have broken apart, that whole of which we have no knowledge because such knowledge could be given only in instinct, and knowledge is only possible in intuition. Wholeness, the integrity of subject and object, is a condition of the absence of knowledge. Knowledge is knowledge of things whose condition of being known is their separation from their unknowable integrity as things in themselves and their representation as things in appearance.

> And we: spectators, always, everywhere,
> turned toward the world of objects [vii]

QUALITY

If one were to make an evolutionary construction of how a lot of originally chaotic pure experiences became gradually differentiated into an orderly inner and outer world, the whole theory would turn upon one's success in explaining how or why the quality of an experience, once active, could become less so, and, from being an energetic attribute in some cases, elsewhere lapse into the status of an inert or merely internal 'nature'.
William James, *Does 'Consciousness' Exist?*

Within the description of the category he calls *Quality*, Kant proposes degrees of magnitude of intensity of perception by which we distinguish the real from the possible. In the first instance, the real is connected directly to sensation and the object in the material world through the agency of which sensation arises. The real can always be established *a posteriori* as something given in experience. On the other hand, there are those things which are not given in experience but exist as possibilities, exist potentially as possible experiences whose possibility can only be given *a priori* as anticipations. Between that which is real and that which is not real lie degrees of intensity, 'a continuity of possible realities and of possible smaller perceptions.'

These qualitative judgments of the understanding of just how much of the extension of experience is given as idea or imagination, are anticipated in the animal's world of instinctive behaviour. In evolution, repeated exposure to particular sensations has reinforced habitual instinctive forms of behaviour, none of which requires as the condition of its efficacy its form of representation. This is more apparent and easier to understand if we avoid examples of visual perceptions as the main source of information about the world, since we soon start to recreate in our own heads the representational world of our perceptions and impose these on the animal's world. Some fishes create electromagnetic fields around them, and it is disturbances in that field that create the impressions of external activity to which they are responsive. The echo location techniques of the bat allow it to locate prey and avoid obstacles, showing fine discrimination between objects of different interests. The mole finds its subterranean way with its sensitive snout. The perceptual world of the tick is described by Jakob von Uexküll in his book *Umwelt und Innenwelt der Tiere* (1909):

> After mating, the female climbs to the tip of a twig on some bush. There she clings at such a height that she can drop on small mammals that may run under her, or be brushed off by larger animals. The eyeless tick is directed to this watchtower by a general photosensitivity of her skin. The

approaching prey is revealed to the blind and deaf highway woman by her sense of smell. The odour of butyric acid that emanates from the skin glands of all mammals, acts on the tick as a signal to leave her watchtower and hurl herself down. If, in doing so, she lands on something warm – a fine sense of temperature betrays this to her – she has reached her prey, the warm-blooded creature. It only remains for her to find a hairless spot. There she burrows deep into the skin of her prey and slowly pumps herself full of warm blood. Experiments with artificial membranes and fluids other than blood have proved that the tick lacks all sense of taste. Once the membrane is perforated, she will drink any fluid of the right temperature.

What characterises all these examples is the immediacy of sensation, of the actual presence of an object as a source of sensation in the material world, and the immediacy or integrity of action or reaction on the part of the organism. At its most intense it might justifiably be described as at its most real, in the sense that object and sensation are both presented for action. This is what, in natural language, we mean by real – that objects exist as objects of sensation and attention and, moreover, exist shaped to our need to act upon them or to take action in response to our apprehension of them. They are not merely objects of contemplation. The real has a given maximum intensity, for it is the real with which we are daily engaged as objects of necessity and vital importance. However, not everything in the animal's world is given in such intensity, and therefore not every object given is given in reality. Some objects are given in anticipation or potentiality, but always potentially for action and therefore potentially real. In behaviour, while it is directly concerned with an object of intensity we could describe the condition of the organism as being in 'active subjective mode,' that is, immediately concerned and occupied in attention with those matters of immediate importance to itself. But, like the dog asleep with one eye open, the animal has its inactive subjective mode where it is not directly and immediately engaged with its sensations and perceptions of the material world, but rests in a quiescent state of anticipation. The potentiality of the sleeping dragon to visit its interests on the objects of this world is always present, merely awaiting the recognisable forms of its interest. Appetites subside, but will arise again, just as attention rests but can be instantly awakened. Therefore the objects of potential action exist in anticipation just as they exist in reality at the moment of attention, though in instinct they exist purely as nervous system responses in quiescent states and not as representations of possibilities awaiting their realisation. Between the quiescent state of potentiality for action and the active state of immediate apprehension of reality lie those degrees of intensity of experience that might at any moment increase or diminish in intensity as our interest or attention grows or recedes. Not every movement of every leaf in a forest attracts the attention of the tiger, but some subtle degree of difference in their movement will raise the intensity of the tiger's interest, and some further incident of sudden movement will gather to it all the intensity of the tiger's interests and potentiality for action. The possibility of realisation lies all the time quiescent in anticipation, side by side with the realised. Given first in instinct as the potentiality for action, it is given in translation in the understanding as the *a priori* mode of judgment of the possible.

RELATION

this sense represents to consciousness even our own selves as we appear to ourselves, not as we are in ourselves. Immanuel Kant, *Critique of Pure Reason*

Now, the fact that we separate out the thing itself from its qualitative attributes, such as its colour, size and shape, should not mislead us into thinking that there is such a thing as the object itself without its qualities, or that qualities themselves unattached to the object can exist in their own right. Where are the triangles of experience? There is nothing given in sensation or in experience that will allow us to judge of the existence of an object without its qualities as an object, or anything given as an attribute separate from the totality of the experience of the object with its attributes. For this reason, the judgment of the object and its attributes, the thing itself and the qualities it 'possesses' – in philosophy, *substantia et accidens* – can be given only *a priori* since it cannot be derived directly from experience. We have already seen that an object must be separated out from the totality of its integral experience in sensation in order to be represented as an object, and that space and time are the two given conditions of its representation in appearance. Equally, the separation of object and attribute is a step farther in the segregation of the integrity of experience into component parts that, once separated, can only be reintegrated by the synthesis of the parts that have been separated. As with quantitative judgments, this is an artificial representation of something that of its own nature is integral, whose integral nature is beyond our knowledge, since our knowledge of the object is its representation and we represent it as object with qualities or attributes.

We may take as a single, simple example of how such *a priori* capabilities for representation in this manner in the understanding can be derived from instinct, and limit ourselves to colour, size and shape. In the stickleback, the male's defensive behaviour is elicited by the recognition of an intruder of the same species. The characteristics that trigger the defensive response are composed of the proximity of the intruder in its location in relation to the defender, its size and shape, and the exhibition in particular of a red underbelly. All these factors, singly or together, release the behavioural response. The intruder is not, here, a stickleback (as object) with the attributes of size and shape and colour. It is not in any matter of fact way a stickleback at all. It is a collection of potential sensations in experience with the capability to elicit particular responses from an organism equipped with anticipatory mechanisms for responding, instinctively and habitually, to the actual presence of those sensations. It is only the continuity and persistence of those habitual responses that create 'something' as a real and material object. That object is not otherwise 'represented' as an object in reality, much less as an object as something existing in its own right with a variety of attributes ascribable to it. But, translated into representation in the mind, this is exactly what an object is – not the repeated, habituated confirmation of the reality of the object in behaviour, but the separate representation of the object and its attributes as the possibility of all our actions upon it, or our reactions to it, which may be as diverse as those representations will allow and not limited strictly to those of necessity.

We may now see that this habituation of stimulus and response which characterises the organism's behaviour in instinct should lead inexorably in intuition to the *a priori* ability to represent relations between a cause and its effect. In instinctive behaviour we cannot say that the releasing sign stimulus of an intruder is the cause of the behavioural response in the defender. We can only say that there are integrated cycles of behaviour and response, action and reaction. The causal connection does not need to be made, just as objects do not require the prior consent of the concepts of space and time to exist in relation to the organism's orientation towards them. But the fact of habituated responses in sequence lends itself to the representation of connections and relations in time in the mind's representational world of reality, and it does so as the *a priori* condition of knowing anything in a connected way, in

> a totality of connected, as opposed to a mere aggregate of disconnected, notions. [viii]

In the animal's world they are connected in fact in behaviour, but the understanding needs to connect them in their second order representation. If they are not to exist as singularities, forever limited to experience after unconnected experience (just one damned thing after another), then their connections are to be made by translating habituated sequences of responses in behaviour into causal links between the origins of behaviour and our behavioural responses themselves, between the matter of our attention and what we should do.

But experiences simply *are* singularities until we create from them communities of experiences. In instinct that community of experience is really the cumulative effect of one habituated response after another. The habits of instinct are the unconscious mechanisms of economic effectiveness, the nearest the animal has to shortcut means to an end in the absence of the shorthand representation of all its possible ways and means that the mind possesses. It is a strange thing to realise that what brings diverse experiences together into communities or categories of understanding has nothing much to do with the *objects* of experience themselves, but with the consistency and persistence of the experiences themselves. The survival of an individual and its replication into similar individuals has been achieved by the accidental processes of natural selection. But those processes are not arbitrary and nor are the accidents always fatal. If every buffet of experience broke the resilience of every organism then nothing could survive. But the accumulation of resilience is the net effect of failure after failure to resist, so that something finally and continually does resist. The accumulation of persistent behaviour that favours resistance over capitulation to circumstance, of itself produces stable and consistent patterns of behaviour over time. Arbitrary deviations from those patterns, were they possible, would recreate the occasions for arbitrary accidents and destruction. So consistency is the prior condition of persistence. Instinct is economy of behaviour habituated over time.

That things should coexist and cohere as communities of

experiences is essential if they are not always to fall apart, in the same way that the absence of consistency in instinct would lead simply to fatal experiences coming one after another. Coherence of representation begins with coherence of behaviour. The experience of the actual physical presence of a fox will send the hens running. And so will another and another, one experience following another. Each experience is unique as an event, but they remain consistent *in* experience from one to the next. Hens react like this to each and every fox, yet this does not mean that there must exist a class or community of physical objects called foxes. There exists only consistency and community of behaviour on each separate occasion. Such consistency is economical and preservative. Inconsistency, or the ability to act habitually, is fatal. Thus classes of objects are really classes of perceptions of objects whose thread of consistency is the sameness of perception and behaviour not the sameness of physical objects. The 'sameness' is given prior to experience in instinct as the potential for consistency of actions. It is given, in translation in understanding, *a priori*, as the simultaneity or coexistence of communities of objects in space and time that might be given solely as singularities in experience, but never are.

The economic effectiveness of evolution is seen most clearly in the world of instinctive behaviour. We can see that the animal can orientate itself as subject towards the object of its attention without the need of a prior knowledge of space. It can act of itself driven by its own innate appetites and interests, and react and respond to acts and movements in the world of its experience without knowledge of time, without the need to represent any object in space and time in any manner whatsoever. It need not distinguish an object as a separate entity cut out from the totality of its experience of the object, nor represent the substance of any object separately from those attributes in sensation that elicit particular responses. There are no singularities or pluralities of objects that need to be held separately from the range of possible actions that the organism is capable of in relation to them. And its relation to them is formed consistently and persistently as habituated instinctive forms of perception and behaviour. But we can see that the economy of evolution can be revolutionised if we translate all that is given in instinct into what may be given in intuition as the possibility of the representation of things in appearance in all their qualitative relations. Every category of the understanding that is given *a priori* as the possibility of understanding and the ground of knowledge, is predicated in instinct. Understanding can evolve and has evolved from the earlier constraints of favourable behaviour in instinct, and if we are to restrict, as we have, the definition of the nature of the understanding to those exhaustive categories of Kant, we can see that in each case there is a prior form in instinct.

There is one more thing to say. In all this, whether in instinct or in intuition, the organism's interests are in totality not interests in the external world, or in objects, but are self-interests. Its experiences are integral with the world that it experiences, and thus it does not and cannot separate out either the object of experience nor the subject which experiences. It may orientate itself towards the object of its desire, but it is not focused on an object as such, nor is it in itself as such the subject of its own desire. If the world does not exist in any representational form as object in instinct, it is equally true that the object of its self-interest does not exist as self or subject. The breakthrough of self-interest achieved by the conscious organism took with it all the prior conditions of the potentiality for representation which would create the conditions of mind which we have called the *a priori* categories of the understanding. But among the objects of representation was also to be found, for the first time, the representation of the subject, of the self, as the economic form of its own interests. The consequence of the representation of the self among the objects of the understanding has been to create a reciprocity of experience that was previously entirely irrelevant to the instinctive organism in its world. The economy of instinct does not require that a subject be established first in order that it might then determine what its self-interests are, yet everything is aimed towards its interests. But in the economy of consciousness, all our representations are of our own interestedness. Paramount among them is the self, to which all interests adhere. Thus we have created a reciprocity of knowledge that previously did not and could not exist. The objects of our attention exist, as they do also in instinct, *only* because they are matters of our interest. But now they exist in *relation* to us. We represent ourselves as subject for whom the world is the object. Since this is the fundamental relation of self-interest brought to perfection, the objective reality of the external world of self-interest is not a matter for disbelief. It has been too great an undertaking and too costly an investment of evolution for that. The categories of the understanding translated from instinct ensure that the unity, integrity and essentially unknowable nature of the world in itself are not and never can be the same as the representation of the world to our understanding. We know it now, where we did not know it before, and 'knowing' means representing 'it' by the rules of knowledge, which includes the knower as well as the known.

MODALITY

I have shown...that truth is a quality belonging exclusively to judgments. Arthur Schopenhauer, *On the Fourfold Root of the Principle of Sufficient Reason*

Kant defined a fourth category, which he called *Modality*. Within this category he brought together the *a priori* judgments we make between possibility and impossibility, existence and non-existence, necessity and contingency. The impossibility of something and the non-existence of something cannot be given in experience. Yet we are able to say that something is impossible or something does not exist, and these possibilities are given *a priori*, that is, prior to all experience. Equally, we are able to say that something 'must' be so even though we can have no experience of something as necessary, and we can say that something else need not be so but exists contingently, yet we can have no direct experience of the condition in cause and effect of its existence either by necessity or by accident.

However, these modes of judgment can all be seen as modes of judgment transposed from instinct to intuition consequential on the translation of the former three categories and the concepts of space and time from instinct to intuition. Possibility is a qualitative judgment derived from the representation of something as really existing or only having the potential to exist. Existence is a quantitative judgment derived from the representation of something as a singularity separated out from the integrated totality of experience. Necessity is a relational judgment derived from the representation of something having a cause from which it arises as the necessary effect. But these modes are not modes of existence, possibility, necessity in actuality, but modes of judgment of existence, possibility, necessity. It is with this final category that we come to the definition of the limits within which the mind exercises its prerogative of judgment, without which its capacity for representing a world in space and time, a world of subject and object and a world of reciprocal relations, is of no use whatsoever. For it is in judgment that the mind is exercised – of what things are, of whether they are, whether something might be that is not, what must be and what may be, what the consequences of our actions will be, what, in sum, is real and what is unreal, what is true and what is false. It is upon the economy of these judgments that we prosper or fail. Thought is of no use unless it leads to judgment.

The *final* upshot of thinking is the exercise of volition [ix]

In instinct, judgment is optimised as the necessary conclusion of all other necessary actions, either as the consummation of what began as an impulse towards an object of attention, or as the conclusion of the release of predictive patterns of behaviour in response to sensation. In this respect judgment is determined by the economic necessity of prior habituated and constrained behaviour. But in intuition, the translation of necessary instinctive actions into equally necessary intuitive *a priori* conditions of understanding has optimised the effectiveness of judgment by making that judgment free.

REFERENCES

[i] Immanuel Kant, *Critique of pure reason*

[ii] Arthur Schopenhauer, *On the fourfold root of the principle of sufficient reason*

[iii] Immanuel Kant, *op. cit.*

[iv] William James, Letters

[v] Immanuel Kant, *op. cit.*

[vi] Kenneth Rexroth, translation of a poem by Onakatomi No Yoshinobu in *One hundred poems from the Japanese*, New Directions, 1955

[vii] Rainer Maria Rilke, *The eighth elegy* (trans. Stephen Mitchell)

[viii] Arthur Schopenhauer, *op. cit.*

[ix] Charles S Peirce, *How to make our ideas clear*

www.ingramcontent.com/pod-product-compliance
Lightning Source LLC
Chambersburg PA
CBHW050754250626
47155CB00005B/2063